My Life in a Kwagu'ł Big House

Library and Archives Canada Cataloguing in Publication

Jacobson, Diane, 1955-
My life in a Kwagu'l big house / Diane Jacobson.

ISBN-13: 978-1-894778-20-6
ISBN-10: 1-894778-20-0

1. Jacobson, Diane, 1955- --Childhood and youth.
2. Kwakiutl Indians--British Columbia--Alert Bay--Biography.
I. Title.

PS8619.A256Z47 2005   971.1'2   C2005-906364-5

Printed in Canada by Imprimerie Gauvin

Mixed Sources
Product group from well-managed
forests and recycled wood or fiber
www.fsc.org Cert no. SGS-COC-2624
© 1996 Forest Stewardship Council
FSC

Text Design: Suzanne Bates
Cover Design: Suzanne Bates
Copyedit: Julie Turner

Theytus Books Ltd. • *Lot 45*
RR#2 • *Site 50* • *Comp.8*
Penticton • *BC* • *V2A 6J7*
www.theytus.com

On behalf on Theytus Books, we woould like to acknowledges the support of the following:

We acknowledge the financial support of the Government of Canada through the Book Publishing Industry Development Program (BPIDP) for our publishing activities.

We acknowledge the support of the Canada Council for the Arts which last year invested $20.3 million in writing and publishing throughout Canada.

Nous remercions de son soutien le Conseil des Arts du Canada, qui a investi 20,3 millions de dollars l'an demier dans les lettres et l'édition à travers le Canada.

We acknowledge the support of the Province of British Columbia through the British Columbia Arts Council.

 Canadian Heritage Patrimoine canadien   BRITISH COLUMBIA ARTS COUNCIL   Canada Council for the Arts Conseil des Arts du Canada

Contents

Background   viii

Chapter 1 - Big House Memories   1

Chapter 2 - Reality Hits Home   13

Chapter 3 - Play Ball   17

Chapter 4 - Bubbles   23

Chapter 5 - Lessons   35

Chapter 6 - Hockey Night in Canada   41

Chapter 7 - The Maude   44

Chapter 8 - Games We Played   48

Chapter 9 - Deep Experience   55

Chapter 10 - Home Improvements   59

Chapter 11 - Evening Games   62

Chapter 12 - Tragedy Strikes   67

Chapter 13 - Laundry Day   70

Chapter 14 - Past, Present and Future Lessons   73

Chapter 15 - We Are Back   75

Chapter 16 - Native Olympics   81

Chapter 17 - A Fishing Family   89

Chapter 18 - Tradition Goes On   101

Chapter 19 - Sunday Memories   106

Chapter 20 - Competitions and Other Lessons   116

Chapter 21 - Hairy Days Ahead   122

Chapter 22 - Fun and Games   126

Chapter 23 - Sports Day   130

Chapter 24 - Religious Doubts   135

Chapter 25 - Imaginations   139

Chapter 26 - Womanhood Strikes   143

Chapter 27 - Life by the Water   154

Chapter 28 - Fishing Days   166

Chapter 29 - Phil Moves On   173

Chapter 30 - School Daze   178

Chapter 31 - A Sister Arrives   180

Conclusion   187

My Life in a Kwagu'ł Big House

Diane "Honey" Jacobson

Theytus Books Ltd.
Penticton, B.C.

Background

My story is about one of the last families to live in a semi Big House. I come from a very large family. My mother had five sisters and six brothers. My father's mother was no slouch either because my paternal grandmother had four daughters and seven sons so this partially explains why I was lucky enough to grow up in one of the last Big Houses.

Now let's get back to me: I have a one and ONLY brother and one sister along with one very special adopted sister (I will explain the capitalized ONLY later in this story).

My grandfather built this huge white building with four floors on the REZ after the old style Big Houses were torn down and the English were trying to make us natives become farmers, even though fishing was what we were all about.

The day I was born, my father ran into the hospital with baseballs and soccer balls. Imagine his disappointment when he saw I was a girl. Mind you, he won in the end because he made me into one major tomboy.

Now back to the Big House. When Mom and Dad took me home to our Big House, I had grandparents, aunts, uncles and cousins galore waiting to pinch my big chubby cheeks. The house belonged to my dad's family and at any given moment there would be at least twenty to thirty family members living in the home. My dad was the youngest son out of the eleven so we rated a cute little suite on the third floor. It consisted of one bedroom, a small living room with an even smaller kitchen (no washroom, that was a communal fact all of us had to deal with on a daily basis).

By the way, when I say the Big House had four floors, that is a bit misleading because the first floor was the basement where the wood furnace which Uncle Clarence (better known as Uncle Ass) kept stoked throughout the night and all the firewood was kept to heat us. The second floor consisted of a very large living room and kitchen that fed all family members. This same floor had three bedrooms and the one and only washroom with one extra room, which was the ubatalił (pantry). There was another short hallway leading into the kitchen where Granny kept her Ḵawas (dried salmon) in ten-gallon drums. After our family took up a large section of the third floor, there were five other bedrooms. The last floor was a huge attic that was unfinished and more or less was where we kept our keepsakes (junk). I think I have given you enough of a visual picture to say that we did bump into each other quite often in the family abode.

Ages in the Big House varied from newborn to seventy plus. During my early years, all the elders treated each and every child as a special person as long as we showed respect back. I remember being so scared of my grandfather because he looked like a giant that even my father was afraid of. To this day, I barely remember speaking to him. Granny was a totally different story, she joked and teased with all the kids because the majority of us could not speak kwaǩwala

My story about a Kwagu'ł Big House takes place when I was between the ages of six and fifteen. There may be some confusion because many of us had the same first name; we were named after living relatives and we also had nicknames. I will try my best to clarify this throughout. Some things may not have happened in the exact order as they are written here but they did all happen this way to the best of my recollection. When in doubt of certain facts, I went to ask others that lived in the Big House during this time period.

Families living in the Big House during the time period of this story were, oldest to youngest;

1. Grampa Moses and Granny Aẋu

2. Uncle Dayu and Auntie Nora with children Eva, Tina, Vera, Gundy, Maudie, Arthur, Tidi

3. Uncle Ass with children Clarence, Oogie, Bruce, Harold, Leonard

4. Uncle Phillip and Auntie Eddie with children Phillip, Lee

5. Dad and Mom with children Honey, Joe, Cory and Gin

6. Uncle Urban and Auntie Libby with children Donovan, Douglas and Judy

7. Cousins Oxley, Marianne and Toomuch
   *(parents were Uncle Jimmy and Auntie Annie)

8. Cousins Lavina, Emma and George
   *(parents were Uncle Tommy and Auntie Lena)

9. Cousin Bugsy
   *(parents were Uncle Pip and Auntie Dora)

* The parents in brackets did not stay in the Big House but the children did while I was growing up. These other uncles and aunts had previously stayed in the Big House but had moved into their own homes.

Chapter 1 - Big House Memories

I woke up in the middle of the night on the third floor and my worst nightmare had come true. I had to use the washroom downstairs and Granny had told me about the dzunuḵwa (wild woman of the woods) that grabs children to eat them!

I got out of my warm bed and tiptoed from our apartment suite down the long dark hallway. I was not allowed to turn any lights on because aunts and uncles needed their sleep before they went fishing and logging; cousins needed their sleep before they went to school and Gramps could not be woken up because he had to cook for us.

I turned left from the hall and headed down the stairs, each stair creaked and groaned. I got to the bottom stair and turned left, only to face another dark hallway. I felt my way along the hallway, trying to be quiet but my heart was pounding a mile a minute.

I was almost to the ub_atalił (pantry) and I reached for the door that lead to the short hallway and to the bathroom and kitchen area. As I pushed the door open, the dzunuḵwa leaped out of the ubaṯalił, and grabbed me by the neck and screamed!

I yelled out in terror and hit back only to see that it was my older cousin Oogie who had heard me coming down the stairs and decided to wait for the unsuspecting younger cousin.

I quickly ran back upstairs, forgetting why I went downstairs to begin with and frantically cried for my parents. I looked back in fright only to see my cousin roaring with laughter and the whole house in an uproar wondering what the hell was going on!

After tossing and turning from my horrific ordeal I finally fell back to sleep. I sleepily woke up to my dad shaking me. He said to me "Honey, it's time for you and Joe-Joe to go and get more firewood for the stove."

I woke my brother up and we headed down the stairs. We opened the front door and started for the basement. I was not scared this time even though my brother was three years younger then me; I felt there was safety in numbers and if the dzunuḵwa appeared, she would grab the slower chubby one first.

After reaching the basement, I picked on my brother and overloaded him with blocks of wood. I could not beat Oogie up and my brother had to pay the price.

Arguing our way back into the house and struggling up the stairs with our heavy loads, Joe and I dropped the wood off in our apartment. Dad yelled at both of us,

"You kids quit fighting! It's bad enough Honey woke up everybody at 3 a.m."

And this was how one of my days started in the Big House. Mom made us our regular breakfast of mush (oatmeal) with ½ Pacific Milk and ½ water with toast on the side. She told Joe-Joe and I to do the dishes before going to school. My brother was on a chair to wipe the dishes because he was so short. He decided to pay me back, he threw every dish back into the sink saying, "It's dirty, do it right."

Next thing you know the soapsuds were flying everywhere and we were fighting again. After much yelling and screaming with both of us blaming the other one, Mom ended up doing the dishes and told us to head to school.

I walked downstairs and Granny Axu said to me in kwak'wala "Walas Nanu'lu" which meant "really stupid" for waking up the household the night before. She laughed at me because I thought it was a dzunukwa grabbing me. I sheepishly walked out the front door.

After school, we came home and Granny Axu said something to my dad in our language. I looked over and she had a big cedar basket around her neck with three smaller ones inside of it. I asked dad "What's going on?" He replied that Granny wants to go and pick huckleberries. He loaded my cousins Lavina, Phil, Harold, brother Joe and sister Cory plus me into his big 55 Chevy. We drove off towards a place called Sandyville on the back end of the island. Dad went back to get Granny A̲xu and Mom because we couldn't all fit in the first trip.

Granny sat in one area as we started our trek out into the bushes to get branches of huckleberries for her. After giving her the branches, she handed out the three smaller baskets and told us to come back when they were full. By the time we came back with three small full baskets, she was impatiently waiting for more branches.

We quickly ran back into the bush to get more branches for her but not before we emptied the ones we had filled into her larger cedar basket. I looked back as we were climbing over fallen trees to get to the best berry picking spots and saw Granny A̲xu nimbly stripping the branches of the red berries, her head covered by a large cedar hat to keep the sun off her face.

I thought to myself that if we could only pick like her we would be home in a couple of hours. The reality of it was that the majority of our berries ended up in our stomachs. Every one of us would count out how many sweet and sour huckleberries we could shove into our mouths at one time. Mouths puckered up, we chewed them in a wild race to see who would be the champion of the day.

Dad ended up making berry picking a competition so that we wouldn't eat so much of the tasty treat. He said, "Honey, I bet you and Lavina can't fill up your baskets before the boys do." That was it, the race was on because there was no way we were going to let the boys outdo us.

Sitting on a fallen tree surrounded by broken huck-

leberry branches, ravens flying overhead and mosquitoes whizzing all around us, we sat in silence trying to
out pick the three boys. The boys kept looking into our
basket and taunting us saying they were way ahead of us.
Our comeback was that there were only two of us and
they were lucky they had a third person otherwise they
would've been toast in the race.

The sun was beating down on our faces and I could feel
myself getting blacker by the minute. I thought about moving into the shade but then decided that it was better to get
tanned than eaten alive by the mosquitoes. Every so often
the boys would go and get more branches for Granny
Axu, then come back to wherever we had moved to.

Mom was walking out with one of the larger baskets
to empty into Granny's big basket. She was carefully following Dad as he was showing her the way out. They were
walking on a fallen log when she spotted a snake.

Mom screamed and almost made Dad fall off the log
when he turned back to look at her. The full bucket of
huckleberries flew straight up in the air and scattered
everywhere in the bushes. It was funny to see Mom on
the receiving end of one of those looks that we kids were
always getting from Dad and Granny Axu whenever we
did anything wrong.

That one dumped bucket would cost all of us another
two or three hours of hard berry picking. Mom was petrified of snakes and immediately demanded that my Dad
drive her home. Her day of berry picking stopped at that

moment which only slowed us down even more because Dad was one of the best pickers after Granny.

Eventually we filled Granny's big basket and the three smaller ones. We piled back into the car and went to the Big House. There were a lot of huckleberry leaves and bugs in the baskets so Granny Axu made us set up two chairs with a large piece of plywood laid on an angle on them. She then lay a wet sheet on the plywood.

We watched, puzzled, and wondered what she was doing. Granny made a funnel at the end of the plywood and rolled the huckleberries down it. All of the leaves stuck to the wet sheet and the berries ended up in the bucket ready to make preserves and jam out of them.

Joe-Joe and I then went up to our little apartment to peel potatoes for Mom before she came home from working at the hospital. Mom came home and said," Run downstairs, see if there is enough hot water for you kids to have a bath." I obediently ran downstairs to the main kitchen and placed my hand on the huge galvanized water tank, which was heated by the oil stove directly beside it (our only source of hot water unless you count the kettle that was boiled in our suite for individual baths in a very small kitchen sink).

Spreading my fingers as wide as possible from the very top of the tank to see if it was warm to the touch, because that meant some lucky people could have a bath, I quickly raced back up the stairs and relayed the good news. All three of us quickly ran to get our towels and tried to beat someone else to the hot water so we could bath before we were corked (fishing term: someone else lays their fishing seine net just outside of your fishing area and takes what you think is rightfully yours).

Later that night, we were left on our own and there must have been at least twenty kids home alone with no adult supervision. There were also numerous other cousins visiting besides the ones who lived in the Big House.

One of the teenage cousins said, "We should play hide and seek." Normal games were not for us; we found the electrical panel and turned all the power off. Home base was the bottom post of the stairs inside the house and the game was played on the main and third floor.

I was so scared I hid beside the home base so I could be found right away. After being caught, I sat leaning against a wall by home base and watched as Harold went looking for everyone else. You could hear a pin drop in the Big House which was a rare occurrence. Everyone who was hiding was trying to be very quiet and still as Harold tiptoed around corners and peeked behind couches trying to find a cousin.

I jumped as I heard Harold yell out, "ONE, TWO, THREE", and "I SEE YOU!" Loud, heavy footsteps began to echo down the hallway as Harold and "Big Boy" raced towards home base. Harold beat "Big Boy" and it was his turn to count to a hundred while everyone found new hiding spots.

After many games, our parents were spotted heading

up the first flight of stairs just before they entered the Big House. The lights were quickly turned back on and everyone pretended to read or to do homework.

I went to bed but not before I used the washroom because I had learned my lesson the night before.

The next morning I woke up to the smell of Granny Axu's duck soup wafting up from the downstairs kitchen. I felt my stomach start to turn over which was not from the smell of duck but the fear of going to school having to smell like duck. I tried to look sick so that I would be kept home but mom knew all of my tricks.

The long day of school ended but not after I thought everyone kept sniffing me. I felt that the duck aroma was coming out of all of my pores.

Our small town only had one theatre and the movie "Ten Commandments" was showing that Sunday on the matinee. Being the Christian family that we were, all the elders went to the show.

My favourite cousin came to visit me while everyone was at the movies and he thought up this brilliant plan (so we thought). Our town probably had a total of twenty cars on the island and Phillip boy said "Let's throw eggs at the cars going by."

Between the two of us we hit almost every car that wasn't at the show. The two of us hid on the front porch and let loose with both hands, we used up ALL of Granny's eggs. We were laughing hysterically until we saw that we had hit a perfect bulls-eye on my dad's car. Our grandparents and parents were going for a short drive after the movie.

I ran inside and hid behind one of the couches. Phillip boy was trying to disappear under the large table in the living room where Granny Axu did her blanket making and basket weaving. He only received one kick in the ass while I vividly remember each and every one of those seventeen stairs leading to our apartment on the third floor.

The next morning, I went downstairs and apologized to Granny Axu for wasting her eggs on the car. I ended up on the receiving end of that "Walas Nanu'lu" look once again.

The following weekend, Phillip boy and I went to see a movie called "Beach Girls." It starred Annette Funicello and Frankie Avalon. We were amazed that someone could stand on a surfboard and cruise along with a partner singing songs. It made me wish that I lived in California instead of the cold, wet coast of Vancouver Island (action packed adventures and light hearted comedies that were produced in Hollywood gave me an overactive imagination, as most of my family knew). We went home and looked at Granny Axu's old wooden ironing board. Needless to say, I came up with a plan (but not much thought put into the plan). Smiling at each other, we decided to take the legs off Granny's ironing board. Using a small butter knife, we loosened the screws that kept the legs on the board and removed them. We went up to the third floor where I lived with my mom and dad.

Our Malibu wave was at the top of the same seventeen stairs (from my nightmare a few nights earlier) that led to the third floor in the Big House. Phillip boy said, "I'll go behind you and I'll sing the Beach Boys song as we surf."

I balanced myself on the board as it teetered on the top step and my cousin gingerly placed his weight onto our surfboard. Phillip boy stood behind me, hugging my hips and singing at the top off his lungs "Surfing USA." He said that if we leaned over hard enough and left the front door open (which was a bit to the right after the last stair), we could make it all the way to the next flight of steps outside the Big House. Directly across the road was the beach, some rocks and the bay filled with salt water.

I think this was when I began to feel real fear over what we were trying to do. I turned to look at him with my second thoughts ready to spill out of my mouth and all of a sudden, we were off!

I screamed! Phillip boy was hanging onto me for all he was worth. We headed down the stairs and the worst possible thing that could happen, did! My eighty-year-old granny opened the living room door at the bottom of our wave. She had come to see what all the commotion was. She turned right just outside the door and looked up the stairway and saw us barrelling downwards.

Granny yelled, "Ah-Nee-Nee" which when translated into English comes very close to saying, "OH NO, NO!" She quickly stepped back and shut the glass door. I looked down and all I saw was the wall coming towards my face very fast.

I yelled at Phillip boy saying, "Turn your body to the right so we can make it out the front door!" It is definitely not like sleigh riding where your body can control which direction your transportation will take you.

I woke up on the second floor at the bottom of the stairs with family members peering into my face and asking if I was all right. Phillip boy was slower than me to wake up so I didn't immediately get into trouble. Everyone was more concerned that we didn't break any bones or have some sort of concussion.

The punishments came after Phillip boy woke up and I was sent to bed to think of how stupid I had been (even though it was only five in the afternoon). Phillip boy was sent off to face his own parents and I felt sorry for him because I was able to work myself back into Dad's good books quite easily no matter how dumb or stupid the act I did. Auntie Eddie, on the other hand, loved to ground her kids for a month at a time and she stuck to her guns. I knew that I wouldn't be seeing my cousin for quite a while (and once Phillip boy and I were allowed to associate again, a solemn pact was made to never surf again).

The Big House had no television when we were growing up. When Dad came home from working at the Liquor Store (LCB) on Saturday evenings, everyone knew it was him. He quickly parked his beater of a car, noisily raced up the two flights of stairs and carried on down the hall into our small kitchen. Out of breath, he quickly turned on the old radio that had an antenna strung outside the kitchen window. The sound that came out of the radio seemed like nothing but static to me. I did , however,develop an ear for "**Hockey Night In Canada**!"

Dad was a fanatical Montreal Canadiens fan, which was passed on to my brother Joe, sister Cory, me and many other cousins that grew up in the Big House.

This was during the days when the NHL only had six teams and any time Montreal beat anyone, the battles were on. Dad's brother Phillip cheered for Toronto and it made our Saturday night to sit down in the corner somewhere and watch the two of them go at it.

Each of them held back no punches teasing and bugging the other when his team won. Whichever brother's team won, he would be roaring in laughter while putting down his brother's team. The loser tried not to show his anger slowly build under the constant cheap shots about his goalie, his players and how his team would never win the Stanley Cup again.

By this time, it was getting late. We were sent to bed early even though it was still daylight and summertime. Joe and I would be underneath the covers jealously talking about our other cousins who we could hear running around outside playing hide and seek.

Chapter 2 - Reality Hits Home

The Big House wasn't just all fun and play. I remember that an older cousin named Maudie (nickname for Margaret) had just been to the dentist that day. I was on my way to the washroom that night and saw her lying on one of Granny's couches in a great deal of pain. There seemed to be no one up but Maudie and I said goodnight as I passed the living room door on my way back upstairs.

I woke up to a lot of activity and people running around in a panic. I ran to the far side of the Big House by cousin Gundy's bedroom and looked out the window. There was a house fire at one of our family homes less then 200 feet behind the Big House.

I ran downstairs with none of my aunts, uncles, parents or grandparents paying any attention to me because there was chaos everywhere. I stood in the downstairs living room and saw Granny Axu enter from the kitchen back door carrying one of the young boys who lived in that house. She gently lay our cousin onto one of the couches and started to give mouth-to-mouth resuscitation to him.

My cousin looked very pale and his eyes were closed. There was a distinct odour of smoke coming off Granny's clothing and hair but it didn't smell like the smoke I was used to. There wasn't that comforting feeling I got when we were barbecuing fish or when we sat around the small wood stove in the living room.

I thought to myself we had just been playing with him and his brother the day before. Someone older than me finally noticed me. She walked me back upstairs to bed because it was not for young eyes to be seeing what I had just witnessed. I pretended to go to bed but as soon as the older person left, I went back to the window at the side of the house and watched the firemen put out the fire. Everyone was screaming and crying while they stood outside the burning building, waiting to see if anyone else would come out of the fire alive. Husbands and brothers were hugging the women standing around the road that led to the back of the Big House.

I couldn't believe the black smoke that was pouring out from the roof. Glass was being shattered and more flames shot out of the exposed windows. I wanted to leave but was mesmerized by the scene in front of me. I started to cry silent tears and shivered all over.

I cried even harder when I heard the ambulance siren getting closer and closer to our house. Standing by the window, I heard the door downstairs open and knew that the ambulance was here to pick up our cousin who was still lying on one of Granny's couches.

My emotions were in turmoil and I couldn't stand there anymore. I ran to our apartment and crawled into bed with my brother Joe who was still asleep. For some reason, I did not want to be alone. I knew that he wasn't awake but I felt better just lying beside him.

Even though Joe and I fought a lot, he was a comfort to me that night and I wondered what it would be like if he wasn't around anymore. I sensed there was no way that anyone else could come out of that inferno alive.

I went to sleep but had awful nightmares and kept jerking awake. Each time, I tried to go back to sleep, wishing that the fire was just one of my many nightmares.

The next morning, a silent hush prevailed over the Big House. I tried to ask questions but was quietly told, "Not now, we will tell you later." I tiptoed around all the older people downstairs who were in the living room and went to sit on the Big House stairs with other cousins. We sat there very quietly, listening to Granny and Gramps talking with aunties and uncles about our two younger cousins who had died in the house fire.

We were young and didn't fully understand death yet but I know that all of us on the steps were in some type of shock. Phillip boy and I went upstairs where we could talk in whispers in one of the rooms and not disturb our elders.

We kept looking out that bedroom window where I had stood the night before and looked at the smouldering ruin that was left of the house. Turning to each other, we talked about our cousins and still could not believe that they were dead. We viewed death through kids' eyes. By that, I guess I mean not in the same way that our elders downstairs were grieving, but in an immature, questioning way, not really understanding what exactly we were feeling.

A few days later, some of us worked up the courage to walk through what was left of the house. I don't know why but we picked up the phone that was still hanging on what was left of a wall. We were shocked to hear that the phone still had a dial tone. This bothered us because a phone still was able to connect with us while our cousins could not.

It felt too strange and morbid to be in their blackened, charred remnants of a house so we quickly got out of the building after a quick look around.

This led to endless discussions that day about death, which we still had no firm grasp of, and none of us slept very well that night.

Chapter 3 - Play Ball

The following Sunday was another day with the Big House family picking salal berries with Granny A<u>x</u>u so she could make her jam. We all gathered at one of the good salal berry picking areas and went to work. Our fingers quickly turned purple from the berries. These weren't as tasty a treat as huckleberries so we actually picked more of these then we ate. The salal jam was a different story and was delicious on home-made bread toast and pilot biscuits.

After the berry picking, everyone had a late lunch at the Big House. Dad then took all the younger family members to a grassy area in front of the largest totem pole in the world. He had built two small soccer nets a bit larger then the goals that you see used in the NHL now.

Dad always picked a cousin named Harry boy who was a bit younger than me for his soccer team. All ten of us would go downhill against the two of them while they struggled up the slight incline towards our net. No matter how hard we tried, we lost to Dad and Harry boy almost every time we played soccer. Dad would stick his big butt into our faces whenever anyone of us even came close to stripping the soccer ball away from him. It never ceased to amaze him that none of us could get around his ass and this gave him hysterics when we attempted to try. Both Dad and Harry boy had these heckling laughs that really got under our skins!

We figured this was the only reason Dad chose Harry boy to be on his team. I guess Dad thought he was building character for future athletic teams by teaching us to put up with endless taunting and laughter after consecutively beating us so many times.

All I know is that I learned to shield the soccer ball very well with my lower end when I finally played native soccer down island or at our local June Sports Tournament. He teased so much that I came to tears trying to check him and ended up kicking his foot over and over until I sprained his ankle. I thought I was going to get a balling out but he just kept laughing at me. That hurt me even more then a lecture would have.

After another crushing defeat to Dad and Harry boy, we somehow managed to squeeze into the one car. Dad had to pack me on his lap so that I could push the clutch in when he switched the gears. He used his good right foot to use the break and the gas pedals. Between the two of us we managed to drive us to a place that everyone called "Uncle Eddie's" (local Chinese merchant off reserve) and he bought everyone ice cream and cokes.

We all went home to the Big House for dinner and enjoyed potatoes and some type of fish dish. After the dishes were done, all of us kids went outside to play Indian baseball.

Neighbourhood kids who lived on the street (the beach was just a stone's throw away over a wooden seawall) joined in and we picked our teams. The occasional adult and teenager would join in with us.

Elders taught us to try and pick evenly with equal amount of younger kids and girls on each team. Sportsmanship was stressed but WINNING was everything once teams were chosen.

I will try and explain our baseball rules (which varied depending on what part of the reserve road and whose house you played in front of) that defined the game. You could have any amount of players on a team. There was only one base, not three. There was one back catcher and one pitcher.

The rest of the players in the infield and outfield played where they wished, including on the beach if it was low tide. A batter could hit the ball as many times as he wanted and there was no three strikes rule as in modern baseball.

If a ball was hit and caught as a fly ball, the whole team was out. Whoever caught the ball tried to throw it out of reach of any opposing player and their team had to race to home base before the opposing team found the ball because they could throw it and hit you which disallowed you from batting.

Another interesting rule was the tip rule. If I was batting and tipped the ball with one bounce and the back catcher caught it, my whole team had to freeze on the spot. The first player to move was out. To get up to bat you had to put the whole team out one by one. If one player was left at bat, he could save the whole team by hitting the ball and running to the pitcher's base and back before the opposing team could hit him with the ball. We would then all race to home base to retag before someone threw the ball in and hit us to take away a turn at bat for the person hit.

The ball used was one of the red, white and blue rubber bouncy ones bought in any novelty store. Those were more or less the basic rules of Indian baseball.

You knew you were a threat to the opposing team when they all came in front of your face to try and make you move on a tip ball. All kinds of faces and gestures were made to make the best batter move first. Even more humiliating was when someone was already out on your team and your own team came over and tried to make you move because you couldn't hit or always hit fly balls that put the whole team out.

One crazy cousin nicknamed "Toomuch" was a very good hitter who always made the outfielders work for the ball. During this particular game, she hit a home run right into the water and Harry jumped in and swam out to get it to the cheers of aunts and uncles watching from the Big

House porch steps. By the time Harry could throw it back to the road, Toomuch was back home.

The next batter had to wait, as we had to clear the road for a car to pass to a loud chorus of Boos and both teams screamed out "Beach Way" which meant quit interrupting our game and find another way around us.

The game resumed and the defending team had us down to our last batter. It was up to cousin Tidi to save us all. We all crowded around home base waiting for her thunderous hit. Imagine our surprise when she hit a low grounder that was scooped up just as she reached the pitcher's mound by someone in the infield (pitcher mound was a roofing shingle and the infield was the house next door). The game now came down to the "deadly ten count!"

Tidi had to try to get from the pitcher's base to home base before the pitcher and back catcher passed it back and forth counting from one up to ten each time they caught the ball. She had to time her run when the ball was midway between the two of them. You could cut the tension with a knife as the count reached five! She took off at full speed as the ball was soaring towards the pitcher, who happened to be Lee, who loved to rifle the ball at you as hard as he could before you could tag home base. She made it safely but not before Lee aimed and hit our best batter Oogie square on the back before he tagged the bag, which disallowed him from his next turn at bat.

Cheers erupted from the Big House porch because

our parents enjoyed watching such fine play. This allowed our team another crack at building up our 7-6 lead. Next batter up was cousin "Big Boy" who had a fairly good hit, too. Opponents were yelling, "Sucker up to bat" and "Swing batter, batter" trying to intimidate our first hitter. Big Boy swung and hit one way out into left field (a yard four houses away) that Harold amazingly caught and put us all out.

Thank God it became too dark to play anymore so we came out victorious over our cousins on the opposing team. Other parents could be heard calling kids names up and down the street because it was time for most of us to go home for the night.

As we all entered the Big House for the night to go and get ready for bed, the building echoed with the winning team's fans (parents, uncles, and aunts) ribbing the losers that lived in the house about their loss and the losers loudly answering back that the winners were just lucky it became dark, wait till the next game.

Chapter 4 - Bubbles

The long school week dragged on for every one of us. Nothing exciting happened in the Big House. After getting home on Friday, we were told that the family was going over to the Nimpkish River the next day to catch our sockeye salmon.

Phillip boy and I were both ecstatic! We ran up the stairs and started to make our sandwiches, making sure to pack plenty of junk food for our lunches. He asked to spend the night in our little apartment with us so that he wouldn't get left behind when the boats left at 6 a.m. We ran around looking for gumboots and rain gear and packed a small bag with a change of clothes in case we fell into the river. The last thing packed was a towel to wipe off with in case it was hot enough to swim after the day of fishing. All the kids in the house had a hard time going to sleep in anticipation of the upcoming day.

I woke to Dad shaking all of kids and saying, "Get ready if you are going to come fishing with us." It was a mad house as we all jumped out of bed and into our warm clothes for the trip across to the river. It didn't take us long to fully awaken as the cold fresh air hit us in the face while we walked down to the breakwater.

The sun was just starting to come up behind our island as we piled into the aluminium outboard boats that would take us across to our river. Uncle Clarence tied the punt (type of boat) with the fishing net onto the back of our boat and we towed it across to the old village of Xwalkw.

Within half an hour, we were inside the mouth of the river. It took only minutes to get to the small island across from the old village. Thirty family members piled out of the boats and set to work. Children moved all the pack-sacks, lunches and other bags to the highest ground possible on the island. Adults and teens pulled the fishing net onto the beach on the upriver side.

Experienced fishermen piled the net the way it should be so that it could be reloaded onto the boat for the first set. Another boat with a motor was then placed in front of the fishing net boat ready to tow it out at the first sign of jumpers (fish).

This was when we all sat back and stared at the river in front of us watching for salmon heading upstream. Within twenty minutes, Big Boy yelled out "INSIDE!"

Everyone jumped up and Harry fired up the motor and started making a round set on the school of sockeye. All the kids were at the far end of the island throwing rocks into the river to keep the fish heading upstream towards the net.

Adults were at the top end holding onto the corks on the beach and making sure the lead line didn't come up. Harry reached the kids and leaped onto the small island. The running line was given to the kids, who began pulling the corks towards the beach. Older teens made sure the lead line stayed low once it reached the shore.

Both ends were slowly worked in as we listened to everything the elders told us to do (which basically consisted of "Speed up, Slow down and Whoa, Stop!") This was repeated over and over. I remember hearing "INSIDE, INSIDE," from all over the island. Excitement was everywhere. Phillip boy and I looked at each other and yelled out "BUBBLES, BUBBLES, We got them!" in perfect unison.

Yelling bubbles meant that many fish were starting to gill up on the net, which created the air bubbles that could clearly be seen and was a good indication of a plentiful haul of fish.

The lead line was worked in so that no fish could go underneath the net and then we slowly worked the net up onto the beach. Everyone pitched in, pulling in the corks and web as the lead line came.

Kids ran in the water up to their waists and held the cork line up so that no sockeye would leap over in case the cork line started to sink where the majority of the school was bagging up. Laughter was heard everywhere and people were talking all around us.

All ages were knee deep grabbing fish and rifling them onto the small island away from the river. No one cared how wet they got because this was the highlight of every summer for each and everyone of us. One of the veteran seine boat skippers eyeballed the catch and said, "Looks like we caught a little over five hundred that set, gang."

Another set was made with the same results. In between sets, everyone sat on the beach telling stories, eating and drinking coffee or pop. The younger kids rounded up driftwood and started a small fire in the middle of the island. One of our aunts cleaned three or four sockeye and cousin Bruce put them onto barbecue sticks. He placed the fish around the fire that had been started. Everyone waited in anticipation as soon as we could see the juices running down the sockeye and smell it cooking. As soon as the fish was ready we all dug in to eat. After the meal, we went to lie back on the rocks to watch for more fish heading upstream.

As we lay there full and content, eagles were flying in the blue-sky overhead, ducks were swimming peacefully in the river and seals could be seen trying to catch fish that were heading up river. Phillip boy and I tried to count how many animals we could see in the occasional cloud that drifted by.

We were back in business when the standby call was yelled out by our elders, "Entering, Entering, get ready everyone!" Cigarettes were discarded; coffee and drinks were put down as everyone manned their positions for the next big haul.

After a couple of more sets, it was time to head home. Each Alfred kid took one quick swim to get the sweat and scales off of our bodies then an empty boat was pulled to the beach and the day's catch was thrown in. The boats that we came across were also loaded with salmon.

I climbed into a boat and was surrounded by salmon just as other cousins were. We slowly headed out of the river with our elders missing each and every snag or shallow spot with ease.

The boat was so low in the water I could dangle my feet over the edge almost to my knees in the ocean. The trip was slower going home but none of us minded. The sun was drying us off as we watched the bay getting nearer and nearer.

As we slowly chugged back towards the bay, speedboats, sailboats and fishing boats passed by us. Eagles and seagulls were swarming over our heads eyeing the bountiful catch we were carrying. These birds knew that they would see a fair share of fish heads, tails and guts once the cleaning process was underway.

We looked at the breakwater to see many cars and trucks waiting. People were walking down the ramp carrying their fishing totes. The day wasn't over yet. We all had to pitch the fish into the totes; buckets, bags or whatever to carry fish to family homes.

Some family members cleaned the fish on the wharf. After the fish was distributed evenly amongst everyone, our uncles ran our share of fish on the boats to the beach in front of the Big House. The next step was to carry the fish behind the Big House for Granny A<u>x</u>u and our aunties. It was late in the day so the fish were placed into tubs and canisters with ice to keep them fresh and cold overnight.

Phillip boy spent the night with us again because he wanted to get an early start helping with the fish cleaning. Both of us tried to carry on a conversation but were soon in a deep sleep.

Before I knew it, we were rudely woken up. There was no rest in the Big House when it came to canning fish. My brother, sister, Phil and I groggily descended the stairs banging into the railings on the way down. I almost hit Tidi and Lavina as they stumbled out of Auntie Nora's bedroom. Everyone was woken up to contribute to can fish day and our parents had kindly let us sleep a bit longer than the adults.

Patience was something we learned as every girl lined up to use that one and only washroom (boys were able to go outside as we all know). We took turns washing up and began a new day helping with what came naturally to our family- working on fish that would be our main source of food during the long winter months ahead. Our elders started us at the simplest of jobs as children. No one did anything else other than what he or she was told because we had to be taught the right way to do our fish by the more experienced workers.

Lavina and I were sent to the "bucket brigade that washed and cleaned fish of blood crew" which was filled to the brim with sockeye. This was because we were younger than most of the other cousins and hadn't learned how to clean the actual fish yet. Phillip boy was sent to the head cutting/ tails/ guts duty even though he was younger than us because he had been out gillnetting with an uncle who had taught him how to clean fish. He even knew how to put fish onto a barbecue stick and had moved up the chain of command, a fact which he never ceased to lord over us.

While standing there washing the salmon, I looked over and saw that Granny A̱xu already had the x̱alat̓si (means container for smoke in English) going. We were up at 7 a.m. and I wondered how long they had been up cleaning, cutting the salmon to be able to have twenty fish on barbecue sticks cooking around the fire inside the x̱alat̓si.

Cousins younger than us were heading to Grassy Pointe to go and collect truckloads of driftwood for the fire we would need to boil the cases of fish that would be ready at the end of the day. Wood was also needed to keep the fire going for the x̱alat̓si where the barbecued fish was cooking throughout the day.

Others were sent to kitchen duty to cook fish eggs and to put potatoes on. They also boiled fish heads and tails for the hard workers outside. Granny A̱xu's kitchen always had food ready whenever family became hungry.

Maudie, Tidi and many older cousins were on the cutting detail where they used a small cedar stick measured precisely to cut the fish to the exact height of the cans to be filled.

The next step was for experienced canners (elders) who did the filling of the cans with no room for error because a can could be spoiled if the cut fish was not placed just right. The can may not seal right, be too full or end up expanding after boiling, ruining all the hard work put in by everyone.

The very youngest, like my sister Cory and cousin Angie, were the ones who wiped the cans clean and added just the right amount of salt.

Last but most important was the person who actually sealed the lids. This job was left to older people who knew just how many times to turn clockwise, then counter clockwise with the exact amount of pressure on the canning machine needed to get the proper seal.

Inside and outside the Big House, everyone was laughing, talking and rubbing their sore backs but enjoying every minute because we were with family. The cutters had aprons and garbage bags wrapped around them to keep the fish blood off their clothing. Women wore hats and kerchiefs to keep the sun off of them. The grass was saturated with bloody water and fish scales.

Every so often someone would take a coffee break and have a cigarette. The vacated spot would immediately be filled by another family member.

I took a break and ran into the house to have some fish heads and tails with potatoes. I liberally poured t'łina (oolichan grease) over the potatoes and fish, then dug in. Cousin Harold walked in with a couple of barbecued fish hot off the fire. The fish were stripped off of the sticks and demolished in a matter of minutes. It felt so good to sit down after standing up washing fish all morning. As I sat there eating, one person would leave and someone else would immediately sit down in the empty chair.

I went back outside to relieve Lavina so that she could come in and get something to eat. She said, "I'm glad you came back so fast. The barbecued fish was starting to make my stomach growl."

It seemed that whenever the bucket looked empty, an uncle would come along and throw another twenty more sockeye in. I was covered in fish scales from head to toe. My fingers were all wrinkled from being immersed in water all day.

Just when I thought I was going to get a break, I was told by Granny Axu to go and help the other kids dump the fish guts, unused heads and tails down the beach. I made sure that I partnered up with Big Boy because he was bigger and stronger then some of the other kids who also had to dump buckets of waste.

After supper, Phillip boy, Lavina and I sat around on blocks of cedar watching Dad and Uncle Clarence load the big oil drum with thirty cases of uncooked cans. This took them about half an hour to complete. Phillip boy ran to get the garden hose at the side of the house and hooked it up to the tap. He ran it up to his dad, Phil Senior so he could start to fill up the big drum until the water was over the height of the cans. While they were doing this, the rest of us kids moved firewood closer so the fire could be started under the drum. Once the water started to boil, Granny Axu began to time it so we would know when to take the cans out.

We were the only ones around so our next chore was to go back into the kitchen to do the dinner dishes. While that was being done, sharp knives and spoons were brought in from outside for us to clean until the next time they would be needed. We finished that chore quickly because we wanted to go back outside near the fire.

All of us enjoyed sitting around the fire with mosquitoes buzzing around our heads, we listened to the men in the family talking about fishing. They loved to tell stories about their work, their fun nights out and tales about the stupid things some had done. Certain parts were said in kwak'wala when the person speaking didn't want us to know what they were talking about, which always resulted in the ones who did understand roaring in laughter. We laughed even though we didn't understand the inside jokes.

The day finally ended for us around midnight but I later learned that our elders were still up making ƙawas (dried fish) to hang on racks for smoking. The older family members stayed up to cool the cans, which were left overnight. The next morning, all the kids were again woken up very early to wash and dry the cans to be placed back into the empty cases for individual families winter supplies.

Soap was poured into large pails and the cans were placed into them. Phillip boy was loading cans into the soapsuds. I was washing the cans then placing them into another bucket for rinsing. Lavina then wiped them dry and placed them back into the original cardboard boxes. We weren't the only ones doing cans. There were three or four stations set up the same way we were.

Other family members were removing the barbecued fish from the barbecue sticks that had been left in the smokehouse overnight. They set to work cutting the fish to be put into cans for boiling. Another group began stuffing the cut fish into cans. Someone set up the canning machine once again to put the lids on. These cans were then put into the big drum and boiled so that the lids would seal. More firewood was rounded up and the fire was started up again. We went swimming down the beach because it was a nice hot day while the men watched the fire. Whenever we felt too cold, we ran up behind the Big House and sat around the fire or climbed on top of the big oil drum that supplied fuel to the oil stove for the house.

Our towels started to sizzle from the heat of the oil drum because the black attracted the heat so well. I climbed onto the drum, but I stupidly forgot to lay my towel down first and ended up burning my knees and stomach. No sympathy whatsoever came from the men sitting around the fire, just a lot of laughter at my foolhardiness. After soaking up the rays for a half an hour or so we ran back to the beach for a swim.

Uncle Ass had kept some sockeye from the day before and he was cooking it around the drum. We sat around on the beach talking about how good the fish was going to taste when it was ready. After three or hours of swimming we were told to go and get changed because it was time to clean the next batch of cans that would be coming out of the drum.

We took turns sharing the tub in the bathroom to rinse the salt off of our bodies then went to get dish towels and rags to wipe down the many cans of barbecued fish. It seemed like the drum had supernatural powers since it took forever to empty out. We were all getting tired from swimming and all the work we had done for the past few days.

I thoroughly enjoyed every minute of the canned fish days but was glad that canned fish days were over until the next time.

Chapter 5 - Lessons

After school, Phillip boy and I came home to study our homework. The third floor in the Big House had a funny type of wall that looked like plywood but was more like a giant corkboard. I wrote out the times table from 1 x 1 to 6 x 6 on the wall in crayon and started to teach Phillip boy because he hadn't learned them yet. Gramps always said that Phillip boy was going to be a lawyer because he had such a high forehead where his brain was and it would eventually retain a lot of information. He caught on very fast proving Gramps right when I realized what I had just done! I had just written a chalkboard on the wall. I heard Granny Axu walking slowly up the stairs. I thought I was really going to get it this time for writing on the walls.

We ran and hid under the attic stairs and watched her walk towards my giant blackboard. She didn't even seem to notice and went into one of the bedrooms to call someone. Later on, we overheard her talking about us in her broken English. She knew who had written on the wall but was glad that we were learning our numbers. The times table ended up being used by many other kids in the house after that because it never was taken off.

It was too wet and ugly to play outside so after dinner I went downstairs to trade comic books with Harold. I sat down on one of the chairs and started to read a book. Other's joined, and soon there were quite a few of us sitting around the living room reading. Glancing up, I saw that Granny A<u>x</u>u was busy working with her cedar bark for her baskets. She was quietly singing a kwak'wala song under her breath, and it gave me a comforting feeling as I read.

I went into the kitchen to get some hot chocolate and toast. Older cousins sat talking and laughing around the kitchen table. Their preferred drink was coffee or tea with biscuits smothered in peanut butter.

Tired of reading, I watched Bruce and Oogie play crib for a while. Bruce was well ahead and he kept nudging me saying, "I smell a skunk, someone open a window." He smiled and looked right at Oogie. Lady Luck was on his side as he ended up with a twenty-four hand to add to his already large lead. Bruce ended up beating Oogie and it was almost a double skunk. Oogie immediately demanded a rematch and they dealt the next hand with the loser (Oogie) getting first crib.

Phillip boy finally made an appearance and we went back into the living room to play checkers while Bruce was waving his arms around trying to get rid of the smell of a skunk. This bored us eventually so a game of mar-

bles was started in the long hallway just outside the living room. Joe drew a big circle with chalk and everyone
placed ten marbles each into the circle to play a game
called "Big Pot." We all rolled our favorite shooter marble
the length of the hall to see who ended up closest to the
wall. The nearest kid's marble to the wall had first shot
and so on until the last person had a turn. There were ten
of us playing and the game lasted for two or three hours.
I ended up losing the ten marbles I had placed into the big
pot but not after much arguing and cheating by almost
every kid playing the game. We all heard the dreaded call
to get ready for bed and the usual saying, "Go brush your
teeth and use the washroom before you come upstairs."

The next school day was very hot with plenty of sunshine. Dad was on his break from working at the Liquor
store and came to pick us up at the school during lunch
hour. Lavina, Harold, Big Boy, Phil, Tidi, Joe and myself
were all taken down to Grassey Pointe for a wiener roast
by dad. A fire was quickly lit up and alder branches broken then peeled for sticks to roast the wieners. Hot dogs
were gobbled down so we could start roasting the marsh-
mallows. After guzzling our drinks, Dad placed the empty pop cans on a log forty feet away and said that whoever
hit the most down would win a buck from him. The competition of our family life was on again.

Rocks were flying from all directions and everyone
claiming that it was their rock that had toppled any can
that went over. Lunch hour was over too fast and it was

time to go back to class. On the way to school we asked
Dad if he could take us up to the field to play Indian baseball with all the family members. He said, "I'll see how I
feel after work", which was good as a yes to us.

After dinner, almost all of the family went to the field
to play Indian baseball, which was on a hill further down
on our reserve. Other kids that lived on the hill joined in
and we all had fun. It was hilarious to see mothers barely
hit the ball and even more fun watching them try to run to
the base as fathers easily caught them but pretended that
it was harder than it was. My cousins, Vera and Eva had
dainty lady-like runs with high-pitched feminine screams
that would've been heard a city block away nowadays.
They were always being chased by one of us aiming to hit
or tag them out because it was so much fun watching the
way they ran and hollered.

Other mothers and aunts sat around watching us play,
cheering for their own children. Some didn't play because they were expecting children to add to our tribe and
some just liked to be observers.

As we worked up a thirst, one us would run up to Glo-
ria Hunt's corner store which was in her house up from the
field where we were playing to buy drinks and popsicles
for the ballplayers. As usual, time flew by much too fast
and it was time to head home.

After we were home, I went to my room to get my
pajamas on then went downstairs to trade comics with
Harold. I stayed downstairs to do my reading. We ended

up playing "Hide the Pin" with Granny Aˍxu. She asked us to close our eyes as she grabbed a small pin. She then went to hide it somewhere in the living room.

We could hear her moving about as she tried to find a good spot where we might not be able to find it. She finally told us to open her eyes and we all spread out looking for the pin. It was pretty much like finding a needle in a haystack since the room was so big. Granny would say, "You're getting hot" and if you were too far away, "You are getting colder."

Excitement picked up around Lavina when Granny said, "You're really getting hot, hotter!" Ten people crowded around the last spot that Lavina had been looking at. Granny kept laughing and telling us hot or cold because we were coming so close but still couldn't find the pin.

It was so frustrating because we knew that we were within a foot or two of the pin. The problem was that it could be on the floor, inside a book, on a chair or even behind a picture frame. Another problem was that there were too many of us in one area and we didn't know which one of us Granny meant when she said, "HOTTER, HOTTER."

Lavina found it when she pricked herself on the pin after picking up a magazine on a side table. It was now her turn to hide the pin and she told us to close our eyes.

We played this game until Granny Aˍxu switched to "Spin the Plate." A heavy duty kitchen plate was grabbed from the kitchen and Granny went first. She stood in the middle of the room and spun the plate then called out Tidi's name. She dashed from her chair and tried to grab the plate before it fell to the floor. Granny A<u>x</u>u had sneakily timed her name calling so that it would fall before Tidi could reach it and she had to sing, tell a joke, or a story. She ended up telling a joke and it was now her turn to spin the plate and call anyone of us up to try and catch it before the plate fell over.

Tidi called me next because she knew I was shy and didn't like to do anything in public. I never ran so fast in my life when she yelled, "Honey!"

I just made it before the plate went over and was able to avoid the embarrassment of stuttering and muttering under my breath while attempting to sing or tell a joke. Since I had caught the plate, it was my turn to call on someone. This game lasted until it was time for us to get ready for bed.

I tried to race to the washroom but as usual, was beaten by taller and older cousins. It was a blessing and a curse at the same time. I had to use the washrom but it extended the time before I had to go to bed. Mom started to call for me so I had to head upstairs to put on my bedtime clothes and kiss them goodnight.

Chapter 6 - Hockey Night in Canada

One afternoon after spending my day swimming on the beach, I went home to find no one on the main floor. I went upstairs to see everyone ohhing and ahhing over our new black and white television set! We were one of the first ones to get a television in the village.

It was a Saturday afternoon and mom cooked hamburgers and hot dogs for dinner. Everyone in the Big House was crowded into our apartment suite waiting in great anticipation for "Hockey Night In Canada". The Leafs were playing the Canadiens and fireworks were more or less guaranteed no matter what the outcome. Dad was fiddling around with the antennae, which was outside of the building, trying to get the best possible reception for the big game.

None of us cared that it was in black and white, that there were three players skating in on a breakaway on goal and it looked like they were playing in a snowstorm. I was watching my idol "Gump" Worsley warming up and playing in goal for the Canadiens! The family divided up into their cheering sections, Toronto on one side and Montreal on the other side.

Dad was teasing me, calling my Gump fat and roly-poly. He kept saying that Rogatien Vachon should be the starting goalkeeper for our team. Toronto fans were yelling that Montreal was going down, big time and "OH Canada" hadn't even been sung yet. Dad replied, "How many Stanley Cups does Toronto Maple Leafs have? I know that the Habs are well past twenty, guys!"

The room was buzzing with excitement as the puck was dropped to start the first period and we watched our idols playing live for the first time ever. Announcer Foster Hewitt was still in his prime and each time he raised his voice on an exciting rush, he had us hollering for every close save, every bone crushing hit and every tape-to-tape pass.

I finally saw what I was only able to hear on the radio and that was, "Jean Believeau SHOOTS, HE SCORES!" Our living room erupted with Montreal fans cheering and giving each other high fives. Dad lost his balance and flipped over in his rocking recliner as he leapt up with arms raised to the ceiling. We broke out in laughter as all we saw were his short legs pumping up and down. Pushing and shoving was going on all over the room as Montreal fans started to rub it in to the Toronto fans.

Our joy was short lived because Dave Keon tied up the game within two minutes and the shoe was now on the other foot. If looks could kill, Dad's glare would have dropped Uncle Phil on the spot. Uncle was thoroughly enjoying bugging Dad after the tying goal. Dad could dish it out but not take the teasing back.

During the first intermission, Mom popped some popcorn in a pot on the wood stove and heaped it with butter. Bowls were handed out to anyone who wanted any and Dad poured kool-aid for the kids.

We all raced back to get a good seat for the second period after the filling snack. Bickering amongst the fans started in earnest when Frank Mahovolich scored for the Maple Leafs. Dad was really fuming now as all the Toronto fans got on the Montreal fans case.

The game went back and forth but ended up in a three-three tie, which was fortunate because I don't know if Granny Axu would've been able to stop the warfare amongst the family members. It was a fitting way for the game to end our first day with a television set.

Chapter 7 - The Maude

It was Mom and Dad's Wednesday league bowling night and Maudie was called up from downstairs to sit for us (from previous stories, I don't need to explain why we needed a sitter in a household of thirty plus).

Older cousin Maudie was my favorite sitter because she was a big kid herself in a lot of ways. My brother Joe and sis Cory had already fallen asleep so Maudie asked if I wanted to play soccer in the living room in our suite. Of course I said yes and after many outstanding saves she blasted one past me. There was one major problem, though. After the ball snuck by me, it had crashed through the living room window and down two floors onto the front lawn. We looked at each other in shock because bowling would be over in less than half an hour.

She told me to go and get the ball. I sprinted out the door, ran down the hall and leaped every third step on the stairs. Quickly opening the front door, I ran down the next flight of stairs to get the ball while Maudie was trying to come up with some plausible excuse to tell my parents for

why the window was broken. After I made my way back
upstairs, I held the dustpan for the Maude while she swept
the shards of broken glass into it. She quickly disposed of
the evidence into a garbage can.

Once again, my one and only brother came through.
Maudie told me to go to bed and pretend to be asleep. I
lay beside my innocent brother on our bed in the living
room with my eyes tightly closed when Mom and Dad
came in.

I heard Maudie say, "I feel really bad but I went to the
washroom downstairs and came back just when Wisa (little) Joe accidentally kicked the soccer ball out the window." I lay there with a guilty conscience wondering how
Maudie was sleeping that night because I was tossing and
turning before I fell asleep. Joe never had to face any punishment because of his young age and his being the one and
only brother/son, which thankfully saved Maudie and me.

There were other times that Maudie sat for us and one
night really sticks in my mind. As I mentioned earlier, she
was my favorite sitter but one night she hurt my feelings.
I can laugh at now as I look back on it.

Mom and Dad kissed us all goodnight before they went
bowling and said, "Behave yourselves this time kids."
Maudie and I looked at each other with a twinge of a conscience because we both knew that was directed at Joe
through no fault of his own.

I finished doing the supper dishes and then we all
played a card game called Crazy Eights. Later, Maudie

sent my brother and sister to bed. Being older I was allowed to stay up a bit longer so Maudie braided my hair into two pigtails to kill some time while she babysat.

She then called me into the kitchen to help me make our lunches for the next school day. I was buttering one side of the bread with butter and Maudie was getting the mustard out of the fridge to butter the other slice. She casually walked over to me and held the full jar of mustard over my head thinking it was thick like peanut butter.

The next thing I knew, mustard was pouring down across my face. My eyes began to sting as the mustard hit my eyelashes and quickly seeped inside past my eyelids. I started to howl more in embarrassment than in pain, looking like a Prairie Indian with war paint on. I couldn't see what was happening on the back of my head, but the mustard was rapidly trickling down both of the braids Maudie had just put into my hair. I thought Harry and Dad had mocking laughs but they had nothing on the Maude. She had tears streaming down her face and kept repeating, "I'm sorry Honey" in between each and every outburst of snorting and loud burst of laughter.

She quickly grabbed me and stood me on a small stool in front of the small kitchen sink. Without even untying my braids, she filled the sink with warm water and dunked my head into it. In between my gasps for air and snuffles of tears, she washed my hair with a bar of Lux soap desperately trying to remove the mustard. Throughout all of this, I remember her laughing her head off which only made me cry harder and caused more gut wrenching laughter on her part.

After she undid my braids and did a better job of cleaning me up, she sent me to bed. Maudie then went downstairs to tell the rest of our family what she had just done to me and I could clearly hear laughter even though she was one floor away. I had hurt feelings and was traumatized so I locked the door to our apartment. When she came back up stairs, she kept knocking for me to let her in but I was mad. I knew she would get into trouble if she wasn't in the apartment with us when Mom and Dad came home so this was my revenge. To this day, I relive how I looked that night every time Maudie and other family members break out in chuckles after calling me " Mustard head."

Chapter 8 - Games We Played

My brother Joe had a small pool table given to him as a present one year. The table was about the size of a kitchen table that would normally seat two people and the balls were as large as a giant gumball (we called them jawbreaker gum).

Harry and Joe were having a friendly game when our younger cousin Barb came up the stairs. She quickly asked to play and my conniving brother said that they were playing for money. Barb said she had a bit of money so the boys let her into the game even though she could barely reach above the height of the table. Joe and Harry were much better players and they eventually cleaned her out of her small stash.

Barb was having fun even though she was losing consecutive games so she ended up running off to get her piggy bank. The boys started to let her win the occasional game, which I think, was deliberate so she wouldn't quit playing. She went home with an empty piggy bank by the time they quit playing pool. Joe and Harry ended up spending the rest of the day sitting outside of Cranmer's Pool Hall buying candy, gum, and pop.

The next day Phillip boy and I decided to play some basketball. The front porch of the Big House was enclosed and was 10 feet by 15 feet wide. Running across the length of the porch 10 feet above the front door was a two by four projecting outwards. This is where we played basketball. Everyone of us had an imaginary basketball hoop placed dead center of that board, a sort of gentlemen's agreement amongst us that we all pretty much abided by. Our basketball was anything that happened to be on hand. Things that we used for a ball could be two pairs of socks tightly tied together, a jack ball, a small rubber ball or any thing that remotely had a bit of bounce in it and closely resembled a ball shape.

Our court was so small that we only played two against two but many games of one on one were played also. On this particular day, Phillip boy and I were going head to head with our less then bouncy sock ball. Using his imaginary dribble (sock wouldn't bounce for us), Phil drove by me and did a lay up which I tried to jump and block. It hit the right spot off the backboard and counted for two. It was now my turn to try and get past Phil and as I stepped around him, he somehow got his hand on the ball and stuffed me perfectly. The game went back and forth with Phil leading 28-24 when I went up for a jump shot. I hit for two points but the game was delayed while we took a t.v. timeout (the sock was stuck on the two by four ledge and we had to run inside to get the broom to knock it off). Once the game resumed, I ended up rejecting one of Phillip boy's shots and knocked it out of bounds and it slowly rolled down the Big House stairs into a mud puddle down by the road. We ended up fighting over who had to go and get the ball. I said he should because it was now his possession. He said I should because I hit it down the stairs. Being stubborn (probably something we inherited from our fathers), we both would not give in and the sock stayed in the puddle, abruptly ending the game.

We went inside and found Joe and Barb playing cards downstairs. After getting something to drink from Granny A<u>x</u>u's fridge, Phillip boy asked if I wanted to play volleyball but I didn't feel like it. Barb overheard Phillip boy and wanted to know if they could join in. Joe went looking for Lee so he could be the fourth player.

Phillip boy set up the reassembled ironing board at the top of the stairs where the biggest floor space was. I went to our apartment to get Barb more socks that she tied together for their volleyball. I made the outline for the court on the wooden floor with chalk. Even though the net was only four feet high, everyone enjoyed playing volleyball with those old socks.

Lee showed up and I sat down to watch the game. The four of them played paper, scissor, and rock to see who would partner up with whom on the court. The teams divided into Barb and Joe against the two brothers. After a coin toss, Barb had first serve.

Since volleyballs don't have to bounce, the players didn't need to pretend as much as in the basketball games. It seemed more realistic to the participants and any fans watching. I sat on a pillow on one of the railings at the top of the stairs watching the heated action. The play went back and forth with many excellent rallies by both teams. I volunteered to run down the stairs if the ball happened to get hit down the steps. This immediately happened, making me regret my rash statement.

The best thing that could have happened for Joe and Barb's team was that Phillip boy and Lee were partners. The two brothers were so much alike it wasn't funny. Besides being very competitive, they both assumed they were always right if anything went wrong. When Phil made an error during the game, Lee immediately thought Phil should have gotten the ball back into play. Phil quickly blamed Lee for giving such an easy hit for Barb to slam down past Phil. They ended up giving each other that, "I would've had that ball over the net" look throughout the game.

The score came down to "Possible Game" with Joe and Barb at 14 and the brothers stuck at 11. Joe put the ball into the air for his serve, which flew accross so fast that Lee had to make an awesome dive to dig the ball back up. Phill was then able to send the ball flying back across the court but Barb easily bumped the ball for Joe. Joe then spiked the ball down on the other side of the court for the win. Barb and Joe erupted with cheers for themselves and then directed jeers at their opponents.

After a few more games, everyone decided to go and get some snacks downstairs. I went to get drinks while everyone else dug into Granny Axu's big ten-gallon drums of dried k̓awas in the hallway outside the kitchen. We all sat around the table in the kitchen enjoying our snacks. There was an aroma of homemade bread in the room and a fresh batch was in the oven.

I went into the living room to read while everyone else began a game of Monopoly. Granny Axu called me over and asked me to hold her strands of wool while she rolled it into a ball for later use. After I finished helping with the wool, she placed the new ball into the basket beside her. She then bent over to pick up her needles and continued working on her latest knitting project, softly humming a song. On top of Granny's fake fireplace, her old clock announced the time with a "Cuckoo, Cuckoo".

I went back to reading my book and noticed that the other three were quietly playing Monopoly without the usual arguing. I realized why they were getting along. It was because they were in the living room and were being respectful to Granny Axu. They also didn't want to disturb the other people in the room who were reading newspapers, magazines and books.

Every so often, Clarence boy would read out a passage from the sports section on how the Montreal Canadiens were doing to any interested fans near him. Quiet conversations could be heard in the living room and more boisterous talking among the card playing family members in the kitchen. The radio could also be heard in the kitchen playing old time rock and roll.

As I look back on these Big House days, I now see that we were all gaining knowledge in many different areas. As we played sports and games, minds developed and bodies were getting exercise. The older kids taught the younger ones new games such as checkers, chess, monopoly and crib. The games taught us basic arithmetic, how to count money and how to use strategic moves. Respect for others was being learned from older cousins who set the example for the rest of us while sitting in the main living room with Granny and Gramps. Discussions were always going on concerning what we may have read, what was going on around our reserve and government issues that could possibly affect us. Most times, the conversations occurred around us and didn't include us but we were listening. I didn't know it then but I learned a lot without even realizing that it was happening.

Gramps taught me something that I now know as I look back on the few years I had him in my life. I used to watch him typing with his old manual typewriter on the kitchen table, wondering what he was typing about whenever I went past him. Other times, he would be sitting in the same corner at the table talking into an old reel-to-reel tape recorder. He always seemed to be reading, his glasses sliding halfway down his nose. Other times, he would ask us to help look for his glasses and they would be right on top of his head the whole time.

Gramps found reading interesting and it made me want to discover for myself what the big attraction was. I eventually became an avid reader myself and preferred staying at home reading than going out to play sometimes.

I found out there were many worlds out there that I may never get to see but I could experience them through reading. I found knowledge and was able to expand my own vocabulary. I learned to love fiction and non-fiction equally. I read magazines, newspapers, hard cover and paperback books. While sitting at the table having breakfast, I would read the back of the cereal boxes.

I even read one large Bible that was illustrated with colour pictures showing different things like Moses parting the Red Sea, Chariots from Heaven, and David beating Goliath. This version of the Bible was written for someone my age and I never wanted to put it down. I read that book so many times that I had it memorized which helped me when I went to Sunday school.

Curiosity about what Gramps was writing, recording and reading made me want to learn what books had to offer. I am quite sure I am not the only child to come out of the Big House with a thirst for knowledge that could be quenched through reading.

Chapter 9 - Deep Experience

The next day, we went to the basement to play on the tire swing that hung from the rafters but we were soon bored. We ended up sitting outside the Big House shooting the breeze with everyone who walked by. We saw a seine boat coming in that had been out beachcombing for logs. Phil, Lavina and I ran down to watch them tow the logs to the beach and tie them onto the wooden sea wall. There must have been at least twenty logs in a row.

We ran into the house and put shorts and t-shirts on so that we could dive into the water from the last log. The tide was still quite low so the water wasn't too deep and the logs weren't much of a challenge as a diving board.

Phillip boy went to the beach and pushed a large piece of driftwood into the water. After pushing it out as far as possible, we took turns having swimming races out to it. In our minds, we thought we were miles past where we could touch the bottom but I doubt if we were. Eventually we sat on the small log and paddled around with sticks found on the beach while we waited for the tide to rise.

The log became a raft that we were floating down the Amazon River, a canoe that we were using to escape from attacking soldiers and many other things while we waited.

Finally, the tide was the right height for diving in and more people joined us in the water. Competitions started up to see who could hold their breath the longest underwater after jumping in at the deepest part.

An imaginary line was drawn that we all agreed on and groups of four took turns swimming out to the boundary we had picked out as the turnaround area and back. The first one to touch the last log won the race. Other groups went until we had four first place winners who were in the final race to see who was the champion swimmer. Phil, Joe, Lee, and Big Boy were in this final leg of competition. The rest of us were standing around on the logs cheering for our favorite swimmer.

All four dove in and tried to stay under as long as possible to gain an advantage. Once they surfaced, everyone was kicking and splashing salt water in the opponents' faces to try and slow them down. They rounded the first turn and were starting back to the log in a tight race with Phillip boy in front by a nose. Big Boy started to gain and gave one final push to beat Phillip boy by an arm's length. We all declared him the champion.

We were all having so much fun that we didn't notice the tide was still rising. As the water rose, the logs were slowly slipping further apart then closing up again. There must have been twenty or more of us running on the logs and jumping in which made them separate even more.

I don't remember who looked back but Lavina screamed out and we all turned to see what the all the commotion was. She had slipped in between two of the logs right near the deepest part and they had closed back up. All of us were in a panic as we tried to push them apart but because of our size and the combined weight of the logs, they were not budging an inch. Everyone started to yell, "HELP, HELP!"

Most of the adults who heard us yelling thought we were just having fun and making noise like we always did when swimming and did not come to check on us. By this time, Lavina had been submerged for the longest ten to fifteen seconds of our lives and we were getting really scared.

An older man who lived in a house on the beach where we were swimming heard the panic in our voices and came sprinting out of his house. He came running out only wearing his underwear. Running barefoot along the logs, he pushed them apart and jumped in.

It seemed like an eternity but he popped back up holding Lavina in his arms. She was gagging and spitting out water. He pulled himself up onto the logs while still holding Lavina with one hand. Her eyes were closed which really made me worry. She was breathing funny, shivering all over and had blue lips. We all followed him as he ran with her back to the Big House. Granny Axu took one look at her, jumped off her chair by the living room door and started to strip Lavina's clothes off.

Grabbing a blanket from one of the couches, Granny bundled her nice and tight, then packed her onto her lap to give Lavina some of her own body heat. She finally opened her eyes and started to cry now that her initial shock was over. It was one of the happiest moments of my life to see her open her eyes because she was not only my cousin but was my best friend next to Phillip boy.

After Lavina was dressed in dry clothes again, we sat around talking about how scared we had been. It was a good thing that the man who had jumped in was a logger by profession.

What started as another fun day for us was another lesson, which was to be very careful how we played when we went swimming. Our parents gave us a lecture that wasn't soon forgotten.

Chapter 10 - Home Improvements

Joy of joys! My dad told us he was switching the wood stove in our apartment to an oil stove. My brother Joe and I danced with joy thinking that we wouldn't have to pack firewood up two flights of stairs every morning.

Little did I know that the job only became a one-person chore now. Of course since I was the oldest by three years and a bit bigger then Joe, I'll give one guess as to who ended up with the duty.

The oil stove was easier to keep going but its downfall was that we were on the third floor and that made it too hard to pump oil upwards from the basement. This meant that the stove was adapted with a small five-gallon canister off to one side that needed to be refilled every morning.

A larger drum was kept in the basement where the firewood used to be and was refilled once a week. Each and every morning there after I had to go by myself. I had to carry the empty can to the basement with flashlight in hand because it usually was still dark outside.

The first day I went to refill the oil canister, I

looked over at my one and only brother who was warmly wrapped in his blankets. I jumped out of bed, staggered over to my dresser to get my clothes. I rapidly pulled on blue jeans, a t-shirt and a warm sweater. I then donned a thick jacket zippered right up to my neck. I went into the kitchen and tilted the can over to an upright position. Grabbing the flashlight from on top of the fridge, I grumpily walked out of the apartment and down the stairs. I felt the cold air hit me as soon as I opened the front door. Running as fast as I could down the porch stairs and into the basement (silently cursing my brother under my breath and wishing I was born second), I turned the one light on. Using the flashlight to find my way over to the big oil drum, I imagined ghosts and murderers lurked behind every shadowy area in the basement.

I quickly opened the lid on the oil canister, placed the funnel into it and turned the tap wide open on the big drum. Jumping from foot to foot and rubbing my hands together to keep warm, I almost wished we still had a wood stove so Joe could share my misery. I thought that I was being punished by a higher power because I never did own up to my parents about the broken window when Joe had taken the fall for Maudie and me.

It seemed like it took ten minutes to fill up but it was only a couple of minutes. After shutting off the tap, removing the funnel, resealing the drum and turning off the basement light, I headed towards the stairs and back into the house.

A new tradition was about to start in the Big House. The can was heavy; I was crabby and wanted the world to know it. Every time I took a step up towards our apartment, I noisily put the oil can down, the sound resonated throughout the house. I did this everyday hoping that my dad would get tired of it and do it himself.

Everyone heard it and it became a running joke that I was now the new 7 a.m. alarm clock for the household. No one seemed to mind because it was time to wake up anyway, so it backfired in my face. I sill get teased about my misguided plan to get out of an unwanted chore.

Chapter 11 - Evening Games

We were all home later that evening sitting around in the downstairs living room when Granny A<u>x</u>u asked, "Does anyone want to play Jacob and Rachael?" Everyone said yes right away because this was a fun game that everyone could participate in. I ran upstairs to see if anyone else wanted to join the game. Almost everyone came downstairs, even if they had no intention of joining in because half the fun was watching the people playing.

The elders sat around on the three couches and the two smaller sofas held babies or toddlers. Chairs were quickly dragged in from the kitchen for the other adults and kids sat anywhere they could find an empty space. The older boys dragged the table, where Granny A<u>x</u>u lay her blanket and apron sewing stuff, from the middle of the room to the side so it would be out of the way for the game.

While we were setting up the living room, Granny A<u>x</u>u was in the kitchen getting a couple of large towels. Gramps went into the bedroom to get one of his smaller

Indian drums that were used at potlatches.

As usual, most of the kids were vying for the chance to go first at playing Jacob and Rachael. To solve this dilemma, Granny A<u>x</u>u decided to start with one of the oldest and one of the youngest cousins first.

Vera was chosen to be Jacob and Phillip boy was picked to be Rachael. Harold and Big Boy grabbed the towels and blindfolded the two chosen ones. Granny placed "Jacob" by the kitchen door and Uncle Dayu brought "Rachael" boy over by the living room window. "Rachael" boy was handed the drum and a stick. Our cousins Oogie and Bruce further confused them by rapidly spinning both blinded players in circles.

Vera was facing towards the wall and did not realize it, hands outstretched trying to get her bearings and Phillip boy was facing Granny A<u>x</u>u sitting on her favorite golden chair.

The game began with "Jacob" calling out in her feminine voice, "Rachael, Rachael".

Phillip boy gave two quick hits on the drum and tried to move away before Vera stumbled around trying to find him. Vera quickly turned around to where she had heard the drum beat and took five or six hesitant steps because she still had no idea where she was in the living room.

The living room crowd started to make it harder by chanting, "You're getting closer, reach left, two more steps to go VERA!" This caused Phillip boy to panic and he sidestepped to the right to avoid Vera who was still a good ten feet away. This amused all of us and the kids were roaring with laughter at the two of them.

Vera yelled out, "Rachael, Rachael!' again and again to try to hear where the drum's beat would be heard from. Phil thumped two drumbeats and Vera realized she was getting closer to him. At the same time Phillip boy knew she was closer by the sound of her voice and took evasive action by stepping backwards and three over to the left.

Vera's outstretched arms just missed Phillip boy's head by less than an inch! Granny Axu sat there doing another stitch on her latest creation and was chuckling away at how close Vera had come to ending the game by tagging Phillip boy. I was trying to help Phil by saying, "That was too close, bro."

The elders were saying things to each other in kwak̓wala while they watched which only confused Vera more because she understood what they were saying. The kwak̓wala that the elders were speaking made Phillip boy panic because he didn't know what they saying. He thought they were clues being given to Vera by older cousins that spoke the language.

In fear of being caught, Phil walked right into a wall trying to get away from Vera and she heard the big thud and "OOMPH!" sound that Phillip boy made. She dashed over in that same funny shuffling motion with arms outstretched, waving her hands back and forth trying to tag him.

Phillip boy recognized the sound of her slippers sliding along the linoleum. He dropped to the floor onto his knees to try and evade her tag and Vera fell over him. Everyone started laughing, clapping and cheering for the two who had given us a very hilarious first game to watch.

Phillip boy removed his blindfold and bent over to pick up a giggling Vera who was still struggling with her blindfold.

Shouts were heard from all over the room to be the next two that would be the ones to play. The family played the game for three or four more hours until our stomachs started to hurt from all the snorting, giggling, and chuckling that was going on all around the Big House living room at the different "Jacob's" struggling to find all the "Rachael's" that were dodging them.

Granny Axu finally called a time out and the youngest were sent to wash up to get ready for bed. The kids who were allowed to stay up sat around the living room replaying every foolish and funny thing that had happened in the individual games. Most of the mothers went to put the babies to bed then came back to the kitchen to make a cup of tea. The men were already sitting around the table playing cards drinking coffee or tea so the ladies moved into the living room. As I headed up the stairs to bed, I looked into the living room and saw mothers and aunts sitting around sewing, weaving, crocheting or knitting. Everyone said goodnight to me and then went back to whatever conversation they were having before I had poked my head into the room.

I went to say goodnight to the cousins who lived on the same floor, then went to my bed. I crawled under the covers and wrapped myself up nice and tight. Although tired, I fell asleep with a smile on my face as I recalled the night's activities.

Chapter 12 - Tragedy Strikes

It was movie night for the Big House youth and we were on our way to the Bay Theatre. Cousin Eva, was another babysitter of mine, took me to the 7 o'clock feature. As we walked home from the theatre, we heard a fire engine make its loud, piercing noise, a sound that always scared everyone on the island.

One of the older girls asked where the fire was and they said it was at Moses Alfred's house, which was our Big House. It was about a mile from the theatre to our home but we all raced back. We were terrified, images running through our heads of the worst possible scenarios. It seemed to take forever to run past all the stores, the graveyard and then past the old cannery. We finally reached the beginning of the bay and saw shooting flames and billowing black smoke reaching up into the sky less then six houses away, we stopped running in stunned disbelief.

I felt a sigh of relief that it was behind the Big House and knew that our relatives who were still at home were safe. But I immediately felt guilty because a home was still burning and I saw that it was someone who Granny Axu always said was related to her.

The closer we got to the Big House, the more unreal everything seemed. We saw the municipality's old fire truck sitting off of the road, the volunteers manning their stations and connecting hoses. I saw the pump work overtime by the waterline, sucking up the salt water with the hose that snaked up the beach, over the seawall and up past the Big House. People were running around and yelling instructions to each other.

I went to the back of the house where the fire was raging and saw that everyone looked worried and stressed. Faces were covered in soot and reflected the orange glow of the fire. I tried to get a bit closer to watch the fire but Mom quickly grabbed me and said, "You go get your brother and sister, then run inside to get your pajamas right now. Meet me on the front porch when you're done."

We all ran upstairs to do what we were told, then she walked us over to our Uncle's house which was about a three minute walk, heading towards the Council Hall. I asked her why we were sleeping at Uncle Charley-Horse's place. She replied, "Dad and them are worried that the fire behind the Big House might spread to the big oil tank behind our house. It might explode and the fire could spread towards the Big House."

Auntie Annie took care of us while Mom went back to

see what was happening over at our house. She helped us get ready for bed then sent us into her room to lie down. All of us sat up in bed whispering amongst ourselves, wondering what was happening and if we would have a home to go to in the morning.

After a restless night of sleep, Mom woke us up and took us back to the Big House. I was relieved to see that it was still standing but Mom was awfully quiet and I sensed that something bad had once again happened to our family.

As we entered the house, it was very quiet and my bad feeling only got worse. My stomach tensed up as I saw many older relatives sitting around in the living room with hardly anyone talking, and if they were, it was in hushed whispers.

I went upstairs to find Phillip boy and he told me that three young kids were trapped in the house that had burned down the night before. He whispered, "I was listening at the top of the stairs. They all died."

I didn't know what to think as he was saying this to me. He asked if I wanted to go out back to look and I said no. I did not want to go and look at another burned home because I still wasn't over the last fire I had witnessed.

I didn't feel like talking anymore so I went to my room to read something, anything because I did not want to have to deal with this. It scared me too much and I wanted to lose myself in a story where things like this didn't happen to any family.

Chapter 13 - Laundry Day

The Big House families did their wash on different days, for understandable reasons. The weekly laundry day rolled around for our family so it was time to clean up our rooms and find all of the dirty clothes that were usually scattered everywhere. While we were doing that, Mom was downstairs in the kitchen setting up the old wringer washing machine. None of us enjoyed laundry day including Mom. It was a lot of work having to push the clothes by hand through the wringer after the machine had finished washing and rinsing them.

My job was to carry the baskets out the back door and hang them to dry on clotheslines inside a small aluminum covered shed that Dad had built. The shed had no sides to it so the clothing could be wind dried, and it was often quite cold even if the sun was shining because I was always shaded. If there were a lot of clothes, then I had to hang them on the covered back porch so that clothing, blankets and sheets were also exposed to the wind. The best place to dry the wash was on the clothes line that was strung out from one corner of the back porch onto a large tree about seventy-five yards away heading uphill. The wash on this line caught any ocean breeze and the sunshine whenever it happened to be out.

I used to run back in to the oil stove in the kitchen just to warm my hands over it. My fingers were too numb to grip the clothes pegs and squeeze them open to clasp onto t-shirts, jeans and other articles of clothing. Another reason it was so cold was because the wash was always done with cold water, the Big House didn't have the capability to make hot water for the amount of laundry done by our extended family.

The worst part of doing laundry was the tons of ironing that resulted. Once again, being the oldest and a girl, my one and only brother was relieved of this job. My sister Cory was too young to handle a hot iron, so lucky me also received the pleasure of this chore.

It seemed that I would just empty one basket and Mom would put another one down for me. I had to iron pillowcases, sheets, jeans, shirts and dresses for everyone in our apartment. Dad had lots of green Liquor store uniform shirts that had to be maintained and Mom's nursing outfits were a royal pain for me. The one uniform Mom had that I hated with a passion was a mid-length white one with ¼ inch pleats starting from the waist down. It took almost forty-five minutes to get it just right so that the pleats lined up properly. I would stand there and picture Mom gaining weight so she wouldn't fit it anymore or that I would accidentally burn a large hole into the uniform which would forever banish it into the rag pile that was used for house cleaning.

I didn't have the courage to make my greatest fantasy come true though. I just grumbled and mumbled under my breath everytime that the dreaded pleated nurse's uniform reared its ugly head up in the ironing pile.

One of my worst days happened one morning when I was taking the cothes off the line. I was removing the clothes and I finally reached the last of the ten rows under the shed. I saw that some of my favorite jeans and shirts had holes in them. Almost everyone of us kids had some type of damage done to something. Rats had chewed holes into our clothes and I went crying to Mom. She said, "It's not that noticeable, you can still wear them. We can't afford to get anything new right now. You kids will have to make do until there is money to spare."

I was horrified and didn't want to get dressed to go to school but had no choice in the matter. Clothes were passed around family members in the Big House until kids outgrew them and I was so glad when my older cousins shot up in height and size because I was able to get rid of the rat-eaten ones.

Chapter 14 - Past, Present and Future Lessons

I woke up and decided to go see what everyone else was doing downstairs. As usual, Granny Axu was sitting in her chair by the living room entrance. She was brushing her long hair before putting it back into braids. Cousin Oxley was lying on one of the couches tossing and turning. Everybody else was reading or listening to the radio. Lavina warned me not to sit too close to Oxley because he had been out the night before.

I knew what that meant and sat far away. Before too long, we started to snicker as Oxley snuck one stinker out in his sleep. Granny Axu always had a safety pin on her dress for just this reason. She slowly stood up and inched her way towards our cousin. The rest of us in the room leaned over in our chairs anticipating the rude awakening he was about to receive. Oxley's sixth sense kicked in or he smelled his own aroma because he sure leapt right up from that couch and scampered into the kitchen before his butt ended up on the pointy end of that safety pin.

Granny said, "I'll get him next time" and let loose that

unique laugh of hers which started us all laughing. Oxley looked funny sprinting away from our little grandmother.

Joe, Lavina and I went into the kitchen to tease Oxley about how he looked running away. He should have known better because many of us hadn't been lucky enough to get away from that safety pin. It was a definite no-no when you were in Granny's presence to let loose with that bodily function.

Granny walked into the kitchen with her hairbrush. She walked over to the oil stove and carefully cleaned her brush of every one of her strands of hair. I asked her why she did this and she replied in kwak̓wala.

Gramps had to translate for me. He said, "She doesn't want anyone to get a hold of any of her hair because they might know witchcraft and use the strands against her in some way that could cause harm to her."

Lavina and I wondered how that would be possible. One of our older cousins said that is what the old people believe. She said, "If you sit down with Granny, I'll translate her stories about things that she says that have happened in the past to some of our relatives who used to live years ago in the Big Houses all over our territories. It isn't only hair but other things like fingernails."

We immediately wanted to hear these stories that Granny knew but she was busy at that moment. Lavina and I walked outside to play, hoping that we could ask Granny Axu to tell us all about her experiences of witchcraft the next time we sat around with her in the living room.

Chapter 15 - We Are Back

The municipality was able to lure a tour ship called the "Prince George" to make us one of their stopovers. There was a mad dash to teach all the children Indian dances because they wanted the 'Namgis First Nation to perform at the recently constructed Big House (like the original ones that were torn down by our "white fathers" in Ottawa when it was decided to make us give up our so-called heathen ways).

Our family and many other community members were brought to Council Hall. Young girls were taught the women's dances by elders Lucy Brown, Mary Dick and Agnes Cranmer. The boys were also rounded up and taught to Hamat'sa along with some of the mask dances by Mitsa (Herbert Martin).

The reason no one knew how to dance was due to the anti-potlatch law the government had put into place earlier that decade. Our elders had to start from the very beginning to make sure that the kids were doing it the right way. Tidi and Lavina were about 11-12 years old at this time and were lucky enough to be taught by such experienced women. Mitsa was one of the best Hamat'sa dancers and any young male who was taught by him was also very fortunate. I was too shy and lacked confidence to participate so I never learned how to dance like my other cousins.

Some of the older cousins felt funny to be dancing because most of them were taught by teachers and religious people that it was wrong. Now these same cousins were ashamed because they didn't know how to dance. We all found it ironic that white people who had tried to stop us from dancing and singing were now willing to pay to sit and watch us in a Traditional Big House.

Thanks to the excellent teachers, everyone who attended the Council Hall dance sessions excelled and family members were very proud when they watched them practice.

While watching the elders teach, you could see the joy in their faces and so much energy in their dance motions! The singers were proudly singing songs that had existed for generations, which they had been disallowed to use in public for so many years. Drummers were energetically banging the drums with the dancing elders keeping perfect rhythm with the beat.

All the young girls were closely watching their favorite elder trying to mimic the proper movements, turning when they did so that they would not embarrass their teachers, their family, and their tribe.

The elders not only taught the kids how to dance but what the dance meant, where the dance originated, who a dance belonged to and the proper protocol expected in the traditional Big House when using the traditional dances, songs and regalia.

When the cruise ship "Prince George" docked on the wharf, the municipality was excited because they were hoping for much-needed dollars to be spent around town, and the native community was eager to get back into the Big House to do what was unjustly taken away from them.

Our local taxi company 40-K, along with local people who owned cars, were in charge of getting the tourists up to the Big House. The hastily assembled dance group set up everything at the traditional Big House. A fire had been started in the middle of the building with smoke lazily drifting out of the hole in the rooftop.

Elders were putting the button blankets and aprons on the children. Mitsa was getting the young Hamat'sa dancers ready with cedar bark rings and headpieces. You could feel great anticipation in the air amongst the Kwagu'ł people in attendance.

Once all the tourists were seated, the Chief welcomed all the guests in attendance then explained what the audience could expect to see from our people. I felt a tingling sensation run up and down my spine when the hollow log was struck at the very front of the Big House signaling the first song was about to start. The singers started to sing the first song and the first woman stepped out and did a full counter clockwise turn before stepping onto the dance area. Next all the women and female children came out and did the Kwagu'ł Welcome Dance for the tourists.

Flashes were going off from all corners of the building as the tourists snapped photos. The teachers had done an excellent job in my eyes because it looked like the dancers were doing everything in time with the drumbeats and the singing. This was a very different feeling for me. I was so used to being embarrassed and at that moment, I felt so proud watching my family dancing and singing. I still hadn't gotten the courage to attend the practices due to my confused feelings about dancing but promised myself that I would start soon.

I was learning along with the tourists as the dances were being explained because I had no idea what they meant, who owned the right to the dances and so many other things. It felt inspiring to watch our people do what they had always done in the past and yet I still felt pain and confusion because of my lack of knowledge. After the Big House emptied, I was on a mixed emotional high from what I had just witnessed.

Mind you, there were some downfalls to having the tourists come to our village. If the tourists decided to walk back to the ship, it never failed that they would take pictures of the most run down homes, clothes hanging on the lines and of the scruffiest, dirtiest kids in sight.

We figured that these photos were meant to show that

we were poverty-stricken and ignorant and still needed other people to look out for our best interests. By this, I mean how past missionaries and government officials had portrayed us in such a bad light throughout history and still did. Those people really had no idea what our culture was really about and was the cause of all my inner turmoil.

It really irritated Tidi, Lavina and me when we saw tourists taking pictures because those photos would perpetuate a myth to others whenever they would be shown.

Dad was one of the locals with a car and he drove some of the tourists around. It made my day when he came home later and said, "Guess what, they think that they are close to Alaska. They even asked where our igloos were." Then he started to laugh hysterically.

One of them asked what the breakwater pilings were for and Dad told them that they were there to keep polar bears off the island when iceburgs would float by in the winter. We were lucky to get the pond to freeze up at the top of our island, never mind the ocean freezing up.

This made me feel a lot better even though it was a small victory to make up for the awful photos being taken and how those pictures would be used to depict us as native people.

My father loved to tease when someone asked something in ignorance, stupidity or from just being really naïve (like Auntie Libby who is very innocent to this day and was Dad's favorite target) and these tourists were a godsend for him. Another question they always asked Dad was, "Where are your teepees?"

He had a lot of fun during the summer months because the tourists always asked Dad dumb questions whenever he drove for the cruise ship docked at the Government wharf.

It never ceased to amaze me that we knew more about the United States and the tourists didn't take the time to read up on the areas that they would be seeing on their cruise to Alaska.

Chapter 16 - Native Olympics

Once again, movie night rolled around at the Bay Theatre and we all caught the 7 p.m. show. Once we were all at
home, the elders went to the 9 p.m. show. That was our
cue for the Big House mini Olympics to start. Six kitch-
en chairs were moved into Granny A͟xu's living room.
The chairs were separated three feet apart. We pulled out
broomsticks and mops then lay them across the chairs.
A distance of six yards separated the three modified
hurdles. Every Alfred child knew how intense our races
could be and everyone put their best effort into the organized relays.

There were three teams of four in the first qualifying
heat. Our batons were cedar kindling that Lee picked up
by the small wooden stove in the living room. All com-
petitors removed their socks because there was nothing
worse then sliding into one of the walls as you ran as fast
as possible in the relay. The first three lined up in front of
Granny's chair, bent over in the positions much like the
racers we had seen on the snowy television.

Clarence boy was standing at the start line counting out, "ONE, TWO, THREE, and GO!" All three of them looked like graceful gazelles as they leaped over the hurdles. Big Boy reached the end of the living room first and dashed through the narrow doorway. He sprinted into the kitchen and raced around the corner heading towards the next short hallway. Harold was right on his butt and Phillip boy, being as competitive as usual, was coming in a hard third! Two of them reached the kitchen door at the same time and after much jostling because they both couldn't fit through at the same time, Harold, being bigger squeezed through first.

They quickly came around the two sharp corners and headed into the short hallway before they entered through the next door and began gaining on Big Boy. All that was left to finish off was the last thirty-yard sprint down the larger Big House hallway! Many younger cousins were sitting along the stairs peeking through the railings chanting for their favorite cousin. The batons were passed on to Tidi, Lavina, and Toomuch. As usual, cousin Toomuch was using her bum to hip check the other two out of the way whenever they passed through a doorway so she could maintain her slight lead. Toomuch came in first, Lavina second and Tidi third but everyone was within a foot or two of each other.

Once again the batons were passed on for the third leg of the race. By then the fans were in an uproar, screaming and cheering for one of the teams. People in the living room ran to the stairs to watch after the teams had passed by to see who would round the corner into the home stretch hallway first.

It came down to the final three as the batons were passed to the anchormen, who were always the oldest cousins in the family. This time it was Bruce, Clarence boy and Art. Being much taller, some of us were holding the hurdles a bit higher for them to make it more competitive. Everyone of these guys had taught Toomuch all her sneaky moves and right from the start there was a lot of pushing, shoving and laughter amongst them.

On the last leg, you had to finish off with the hurdles one more time and sprint through the kitchen entrance. After they passed the hallway and leaped over the hurdles for the last time, we saw a photo finish between Bruce and Art. Bruce managed to get some untapped energy for one last push and crossed the line first, Art finished a close second and Clarence boy, not far behind, placed third. The winning team of Bruce, Lavina, Big Boy and Lee were doing their victory dance. They partnered up, banging hips then leaped into the air to give each other high fives.

Everyone congratulated the relay members on running such a close race. The losing teams were saying, "IF ONLY I had ..." which would end in whatever excuse they could come up with. This was one of our favorite ways of starting a sentence after any competition amongst us because no one liked to lose and this was a way of saving face.

It was now time for everyone to participate in the "Limbo" event. It didn't matter how old you were for this event. Older cousins raised the broomstick for younger cousins who would feel good about still being in the competition without realizing that they were being given extra chances.

The old record player was pulled out and the Limbo 45 record was put on. Cousins Oogie and Bruce were the ones holding the broomstick as everyone else lined up. The Limbo dance line was almost ten feet long spreading well into the kitchen because this was a very popular contest.

As soon as the record started its spin on the turntable, each person in the line became caught up in the game and without any prompting broke out singing "Every Limbo boy and girl all around the limbo world. Jack be nimble, Jack be quick, Jack go under the limbo stick..." and the first contestant went under the broomstick as we carried on with the song.

People standing in the line started dancing and bobbing around while waiting for their turn. The first few times everyone made it under the limbo stick and then the two boys started to lower it ever so slowly to thin out some of the players. Smaller children had their extra chances but then it became too hard for them. After the record played at least thirty times, it was beginning to reach the point where the Limbo Dance pros were the only ones left in the line.

This didn't mean that the ones knocked out weren't still having fun. They continued dancing and singing along with the contestants. There were about ten people left when the limbo stick reached two feet in height and that was the cue for Oogie and Bruce to start teasing the players. Their prime role in life was to tease whoever happened to be going under the limbo stick, or any game for that matter. They would both purposely lower the stick just as the unlucky person (Toomuch) was struggling to get past. It never failed to make the participant fall down. Both of them would start cackling and saying, "Is that the best you can do?" to the person flat on his or her back protesting adamantly that, "It wasn't fair, cut out it out you guys!"

It caused endless arguments, which made the game more interesting for the fans watching because witty comments flew back and forth between the complainer and the two holding the limbo stick. The person crying foul was inevitably let back into the game.

Once the Limbo Dancers reached the really low levels of less then a foot or so, the two boys would smarten up. This is when we saw who could cut the mustard and give a lesson in Limbo dancing!

Phillip boy was shimmying back and forth with knees bent and his butt inches from touching the floor. He was making funny looking faces under the strain of the many awkward positions he had to place his body into. He ended up victorious and a thunderous roar erupted from his cheering section.

Next was Arthur (Wisa boy) who loved to limbo and came from two sides of very competitive families. His family loved to dance and he was very flexible. He easily made it through and then it came down to the last dancer left which was Big Boy. He was almost through but you could see that he was struggling when his chest reached the limbo stick. He tried his best but slowly fell backwards and was eliminated. The audience gave him a well deserved round of applause for his gallant effort.

The limbo stick was dropped another couple of inches and this is where the men were separated from the boys! A large dancing circle formed around the final two as the record was restarted for the umpteenth time. Phillip boy was shorter then Arthur and that could be the deciding factor I thought to myself.

I was cheering loud for both of them equally, but inside I was rooting for Phillip boy. It was crunch time as Phillip boy started his dance towards the limbo stick and everyone began singing loudly to get him psyched up to get under the bar. He inched his way forward then backed up because he felt he wasn't positioned just right to make a go of it. When he was ready, he then started his final maneuvers to get under the limbo stick. It took almost twenty seconds but he made it and now the pressure was on Arthur.

His fans started to yell, "ATHA, ATHA!" in the hopes

that this would inspire him onwards to the next round. No hesitation on his part and no backing up whatsoever for cousin Atha; he made it through but with a wee bit of difficulty.

We all were struck with awe at their agility and were looking forward the next drop of the limbo stick. Phillip boy unfortunately fell on his next turn and Arthur would be declared the Champion of the Big House Limbo Dance if he could only make it under the stick. He went at the limbo stick that was only inches from the floor and he almost made it but his head went too far back. He could not manage to raise his upper body back up and that was just enough to pull him down to the floor.

Atha stood in front of the Limbo stick and pulled Phillip boy over and they locked hands wishing each other good luck. The stick handlers played it clean and did not lower either end to make sure that it was a fair finish. Phillip boy went first and fell over almost immediately. It was Wisa boy's last kick at the can and he gave it his best shot but was unable to get his chin under the bar and fell ever so slowly over. We all clapped for the final two contestants and sang the Limbo song one more time for them.

The Limbo Dance was called a tie much to the delight of Phillip boy. As the week went by, both the finalists kept dropping the limbo stick so low to the floor when retelling the story that I doubt if even the rubber man Gumby Phillip boy received as a birthday present would have been able to Limbo Dance under the limbo stick. We politely listened to the exaggerated tale because it was a well-deserved victory by both of them.

By this time, it was nearly eleven so we decided to douse our Olympic flame. We began to get ready for bed because the movie would be out shortly and grandparents and parents would soon be home.

Chapter 17 - A Fishing Family

The family always talked about Gramps being one of the first people to start the Pacific Coast Native Fishing Association. He was one of the first Indians to get a license to seine fish. A school teacher named George Luther who was somehow related to the Alfred and Rufus family helped get the organization off the ground. All of them saw a need to fight for better dollars for native men who caught the fish and for the women who did the canning by traveling up and down the coast in places like Steveston, Bones Bay, Rivers Inlet and in Alert Bay.

The Nimpkish River had so much fish that the 'Namgis people originally speared the fish, used stone weir traps and made small round sets on them. All the fish were brought over to Alert Bay and delivered to the Huson cannery. Native women did the cutting and cleaning in the cannery.

Eventually, gillnet boats were used to catch the salmon at the mouth of the river as they were heading upstream. Our elders were eased out of catching the fish in the river then disallowed from fishing. Without approval from some government agency or a fishing company they could not fish..

Gramps and others disagreed with a lot of the policies put in place so they started another organization called the Native Brotherhood. Its prime mandate was to secure better fishing rights for natives. The organization eventually went up the coast and included the west coast of Vancouver Island.

Gramps also had a herring pond somewhere on the mainland and he used to bring herring roe in for our community. The herring he sold was used for bait and employed family members.

When the commercial fishing was over, Gramps and other Indians who owned boats went to get dog salmon for our community and neighboring villages. Families dried, barbecued or half-smoked the dog salmon.

Granny did her part in the community and was very involved with the Anglican Church Women better known as the ACW. She often had the meetings at the Big House to discuss ways to fundraise for the church. They discussed when a bazaar should be hosted so that all their homemade products could be sold, including articles of clothing made by hand, jams, homemade preserves and baked goods. They never forgot to put a tangle or fish table at the bazaars so that the kids would be able to hound parents for coins to try and win a small toy prize.

Whenever the ACW met at the Big House, Tidi and

Lavina were downstairs and had the duty of washing out the teacups, saucers, and cutlery after the meeting adjourned. There was always a lot of laughter and talking at the meetings. It never failed to amaze me that even while at these meetings, the women's hands were always knitting, doing embroidery work, or sewing something. It seemed like everyone of them walked into the Big House carrying a large bag loaded with crafting tools.

Besides giving back to the community, they gave to us. Christmas was something that we looked forward to every year with great anticipation. There was always a big tree downstairs in front of the living room window that almost touched the ceiling. The tree overflowed with presents for every single person in the Big House. My eyes would light up every time I walked through the room, which was quite often just so I could stare at the expected haul of toys on Christmas morning.

Granny usually closed herself up in her bedroom and wrapped for days on end for our family. When it didn't involve her favorite five grandchildren's immediate family, George, Tidi, Lavina, Harold and Judy were called in to help wrap the presents. They also had to write out the name tags for Granny Axu in English.

We didn't feel bad that they were her favorites. It was just a fact that was obvious to the rest of us. We still had Gramps and many other relatives so it was no big deal to the rest of us. These five sat with her, asked questions, did extra things with her; and she appreciated the attention they gave her and they deserved the extra affection. Most of them were older and more mature then the rest of us. We were still too busy running around having fun to sit still to learn at Granny's knee.

Judy was the only exception. Judy was Auntie Libby's baby and she really looked up to Granny A<u>x</u>u. Because of the time that they spent with Granny, they understood kwak'wala and were partially able to speak in our language with her.

After the presents were wrapped, they were placed under the tree and it was time to get into bed to wait for Santa Claus to come. Sleep usually evaded us well past midnight because we wanted to get up and rip our gifts open.

Christmas finally arrived; children were running everywhere, trying to find slippers and housecoats! The race was on to get to that Christmas tree. We all ran to find out which of the unwrapped gifts from Santa were ours and ours alone.

After the initial excitement of comparing Santa toys and playing with them, Gramps sat on a chair then reached for a present from under the tree. He then called out the person's name and read out who the gift came from. We all sat around in a huge circle impatiently waiting for our names to be called. We watched as each person opened his or her gift then held it up and showed us all what he or she received.

It took quite a long time to do this and Gramps made

it last as long as possible because Christmas only came once a year. Once all the gifts were distributed, we all ran upstairs to play with our new toys. That is, everyone except Phillip boy. His dad had made good money out logging and he was given a little red sports car!

He could peddle all around the living room, through the kitchen door and into the long hallway. He had his own imaginary Indy 500 going on all day long. It was a gift that we all envied and he generously let us all have a turn taking his sports car for a spin.

All day long, other Alfred family members who had their own homes came by and wished us all a Merry Christmas. They sat or stood around with the older relatives as we ran all over shooting guns, playing house, playing new board games and riding Phillip boy's car. Cousins from other houses came by with their toys to show us. We ran to show them ours, then we all shared and swapped for a while. Not once were we reprimanded for the racket we were making. I really think that they were happy to see us enjoying our gifts. Coffee, tea and Christmas cake were handed out to all the guests dropping by throughout the day.

Wrapping paper and boxes were pushed under the tree. That was only temporary because we knew we would have to burn them down the beach in a short while. Parents went to help Gramps and Granny prepare breakfast and we ate in shifts. Most of us kids devoured some toast then went back to play.

Joe went to set up his racing car track that he had received and we all took turns racing around the corners. Each one of us tried to get the inside track because the car placed there always swung out and knocked out the opponent's car in the outside lane.

Dad and Longo came and asked to try the racing set and Joe stupidly said yes. We were not able to get the controls back for over an hour as the two of them were having too much fun. Dad kept saying to Joe, "We'll just have one more race then let you guys use it next." It looked like Joe wanted to beat Dad up because he wasn't able to use his own Christmas present but he impatiently waited. Dad told him, "Longo doesn't visit that often so let us try a bit longer. You will have the racing set all year."

About ten o'clock, the adults started to set up for the family Christmas dinner. The large living room had tables put in place, with large sheets of plywood added as extension pieces. Colorful Christmas paper covers were spread across the makeshift dining tables. Everyone pulled out their best-embroidered tablecloths that were then laid out on top of the paper Christmas ones.

Chairs were rounded up from all over the house and put around the tables. Kids peeled potatoes, carrots and turnips. Some mothers were baking various cakes, others worked on stuffing turkeys and roasts were placed in ovens. The kitchen was a beehive of activity.

We were told to gather our presents and bring them upstairs. Parents dressed us in new clothes. Young girls had their hair pulled, tugged, curled or braided for the family dinner. Young boys were dressed in their new clothes and they were smothered in Brylcreem to keep their unruly hair in place.

Parents put on their best outfits, mothers removed their huge curlers and scotch tape from their bangs for the long preparation of doing each other's hair.

I walked down the stairs with shiny black shoes that kept making me slip. Phillip boy burst out laughing when he saw me because he knew how much I detested wearing dresses and leotards. I tried to tease him back by mussing his hair up but only ended up with a very greasy hand from all the gel Auntie Eddie had rubbed in.

I could smell the turkey before I reached the living room and my stomach started to growl in protest for only giving it toast that day.

Seating arrangements saw the oldest in the family sitting at the long tables in the living room while the youngest sat in the kitchen but well within hearing and yelling distance of our grandparents and parents. Granny Axu said "Grace" before we started eating our Christmas meal.

It was time to enjoy our dinner and it was only on special occasions like this when we all ate at the same time. We all dug in and totally gorged on the scrumptious banquet that everyone had helped to prepare. I thought I was too full to take another bite until I saw the cakes, jarred peaches, huckleberries, blackberries and ice cream come out. It gave us bragging rights since we had helped picked the berries that we topped over our ice cream.

After the tables were cleared off, hot drinks and juice were given to everyone. We all sat around talking and someone brought up the story about the time Gramps did something to get around the potlatch laws.

By this time, most of us kids were in the living room on couches listening to them talking. The government had banned natives from having potlatches and those who did faced a jail sentence if caught. The storyteller said, "Gramps went Christmas shopping and gave every-one a present in the village that they would've been given at a potlatch. The officials tried to stop him and couldn't because the gifts had name tags just like Christians did with their Christmas presents. Gramps said "I am just fol-lowing your traditions, you want us to learn your ways and that is all I am doing."

We all burst out laughing at his ingenuity at getting around the white man's laws. This led to many other fun-ny stories being told around the table by others. While the storytelling was going on, it was our job to cater to our parents' needs. If they wanted fresh coffee or tea we went to refill the cups from the kettles on the stove.

Just as I was getting a sore stomach from laughing so much, Uncle Phillip tried to get up to go the washroom. People started yelling out "No you don't!" Granny Axu then said, "You know the rules. If you want to excuse yourself from the table, we need to hear a joke, song, story or a poem from you."

Uncle Phillip broke out in one of his limericks that he was famous for and did his little dancing jig as he sang. It never failed to make Phillip boy and me break out in giggles. It was a family tradition to extend family dinners to recite something for everyone and it always was a lot of fun. There were outgoing family members who had no problem doing this then there were the shy ones like Auntie Libby who turned beat red and put off getting excused until she absolutely had to. It was funny to watch some of them squirm under the pressure while others thoroughly enjoyed being in the limelight.

After Dad was excused, he loved teasing Auntie Libby. He tried everything to make her ask permission to leave the table. He would tell embarrassing stories about her that made her want to run out of the room but her shyness kept her seated until she was almost the last one at the table. She always laughed along with Dad when he teased her and always said "Oh, honestly Allan Gee!"

After everyone was excused and had entertained the rest of the family, it was time for the least enjoyable part of Christmas. This was the seemingly endless pile of dishes, pots and pans stacked up in the kitchen for the youngest girls to do. The boys were set to work dismantling the long table and returning chairs where they belonged in the house.

Once the dishes were done, I went back into the living room. Card games of crib and Rumolli were just starting up. Others were playing Yahtzee in the kitchen. Phillip boy was setting up a Monopoly game. Tidi, Lavina, Phillip boy, Harold, Joe and I chose our lucky tokens and rolled to see who would get the highest number to go first. Harold was nominated banker since he was the oldest. He quickly counted out the money that each player needed to enter the game. Tidi was in charge of the properties that would be sold. I looked around and everyone was playing some type of game except Gramps who was reading and Granny who was sitting in her chair doing some type of crafts.

The game started in earnest when the properties, railroads and utilities were all sold. Every one of us tried to get the best deal possible for the properties that we bought. I was trying to get all the green colored ones that included New York, Pennsylvania and Pacific Avenue so I could start buying houses and hotels. No one wanted to give an inch as we trying to be good businessmen.

Joe tried to sell me the two cheapest properties along with cash for the red Indiana sections. We all started laughing including Joe because the rent for Baltic Avenue and Mediterranean Avenue with HOTELS barely would cover what I had paid for Indiana Avenue. It was a running joke that this section was considered the slum section of Monopoly whenever we played.

Cousins sitting around watching us kept bugging and teasing. They said things like "Don't do it, you're getting ripped off" or "That's a good one, you won't getter a better deal."

After much wheeling and dealing, the game resumed with none of us really satisfied with our trades. Money changed hands frequently as we placed houses and hotels on our properties. Different sections of the board became like minefields. I prayed to the dice Gods for the right combinations to get me past dangerous corners. Joe and Phillip boy kissed the dice before they threw them for luck. Tidi yelled, "Come to Momma" when she needed certain numbers to evade big payouts. Harold made farting noises as he blew on the dice before he rolled. Lavina's saying was "Come on Baby, YES." It never mattered who was playing, we all had certain superstitions that we clung to each and every game.

Joe ended up stuck with his low rent property along with the title of "Slum Lord" and we were always happy to land on his section because it never really put a dent in our wallets. He always replied, "It's still money guys."

I was knocked out first and had to cash in my money and property. Joe looked at me, smirked and raised his eyebrows in the air. He said "SEE, SEE!"

I took over being the banker so Harold could concentrate on trying to win. The game lasted for over five hours and it kept going back and forth. The remaining three decided to cash in houses, hotels, money and properties to see who was the winner. Phillip boy came in first and Joe a surprising second.

While this was going on Dad and Mom were upstairs

playing their weekly card game with Alfred and Lorraine Cook. The game they played was called Bid Whist. When I finally went upstairs to get ready for bed, it was past midnight and they were still sitting there playing. I went to say goodnight to them and they barely acknowledged me except for a slight nod of their heads. I wondered if that is what we looked like when we were concentrating on our games.

I fell into bed and reflect on how much fun I had that day.

Chapter 18 - Tradition Goes On

Dad finally told me one day that Grampa Moses hadn't been ignoring me all those years as he toiled away on his old typewriter. He said, "Gramps is starting to go deaf and probably doesn't even know that you were in the kitchen. He just gets into what he is typing and is in another world all by himself."

I was able to relate to what Dad said because whenever I was reading a really good book, someone really had to scream at me to get my attention. As most young children, I thought the world revolved around me so I didn't even notice that my big Grampa Moses was losing weight quite rapidly.

He spent more and more time at the kitchen table feverishly typing and talking into the old reel-to-reel tape recorder. It was like he didn't have enough time in a day to get whatever he had on his mind on record for future generations.

Doctor appointments became the norm for Gramps yet he never broke up his daily routine of putting down his thoughts on paper and tape. One day Gramps wasn't around and I noticed that the elders were awfully quiet. After some digging by one of the cousins, Phillip boy and I were told about something that I never even knew existed. To be totally honest, I didn't even know what the word meant and how devastating it would be to Granny Aẋu. Gramps had cancer and our parents were trying to spare us from the despair and fear that they were feeling because they understood how cancer could change lives forever. Many of Gramps' brothers and sisters had died from cancer and there was reason for the family to be worried.

He eventually came back home but it was different around the Big House. Gone was the playful joking and teasing that used to occur on a daily basis. We knew something was drastically wrong and picked up on subtle hints that we had to be less active whenever Gramps was around. All of the kids were not as noisy inside the house because Granny Aẋu seemed to have a shorter and shorter temper with us for the smallest things we did. Parents reprimanded us for any small infraction. Even though we knew something was wrong, elders tried to shield us from what was happening to Gramps.

Gramps was eventually sent to Nanaimo because our small hospital in our town could not meet his needs anymore. The day finally came where all his children received a phone call from down island that each of our aunts and uncles did not want to get.

Granny A<u>x</u>u asked them all to get to Nanaimo as quickly as possible. The doctors did not think Gramps was going to last much longer. Uncles were contacted in logging camps, called from herring ponds and anywhere else they were working. Aunts were very upset as they arranged travel plans for everyone. They would leave as soon as our fathers came in from all over the North Island.

All nieces and nephews were behaving so that no further stress would be added to our elders. It seemed like every person from on and off reserve in our town dropped by the Big House to console the family. The word was out about the phone call and there were no secrets in town like most small communities up and down the coast.

This was one of the few times I ever saw my Dad upset and it made me want to cry because he was the "Rock" I depended on. I thought that nothing could hurt him and it really opened my eyes when I realized that he was only human. To see him try and sneak around to an isolated area in the Big House where he though no one would see him cry was devastating, and to not be able to help him made me feel so inadequate. Men were brought up in those days not to show their feelings and it made it very hard for him to deal with what was happening.

Older cousins and relatives who were not immediate family came to watch over us when Gramps' children and in-laws went to see him Nanaimo. I was not in Nanaimo but I heard that each and every one of Gramps' children made it down island to say their final good-byes to him.

Even though I wasn't there with my elders, I was able to imagine the anguish that all of them were going through. One of our sitters answered the phone in the Big House and started to wail and that is when we found out that Gramps had died.

I went looking for Phillip boy and Lavina. I desperately needed them beside me; they were the next best people to be with besides my parents that would understand the various emotions that I was experiencing. I went from being mad to sad to happy as we talked about the many things Gramps had passed on to us for the short time that he was in our lives.

If it weren't for him none of us would be here. He may not have taught us everything first hand but his children had. We had learned that we didn't have to be the best but to try and do the best that we were capable of. Other lessons we learned from him were respect for one another and others, a thirst for knowledge, how to fish, and so many other things that I cannot even begin to list them all. The ones mentioned here are ones that I recall most of all and I try to practice them to this day.

I think our elders believed in an open casket viewing at home. This is the last time I saw Gramps enter the Big House and this was his way of saying good-bye to us all.

The day finally came and our home was packed with family from all over. There was an endless stream of people from Kwagu'l villages up and down the coast.

Granny A<u>x</u>u was sitting in her normal spot in the Big House and was accepting hugs and condolences from everyone who had come to show their respect for Gramps.

It was too hard for us and we spent most of the time upstairs away from the crowded second floor of the Big House. People were in every room downstairs and were even standing outside on the front and back porches.

Four days after Gramps had been laid to rest, Granny A<u>x</u>u took the scissors from the table and went to cut off her long beautiful braids that she wore each and every day. I asked Tidi why she had done this. She said that, "Our people believe that this lets everyone know that you are in mourning."

Life eventually went back to some semblance of what I considered normal but I would catch Auntie Nora, Dad or one of their siblings staring off into the distance and I knew that they were still in mourning. They knew that Gramps would've wanted everyone to carry on with life for the children's sake because family meant so much to him and so this is exactly what happened.

Chapter 19 - Sunday Memories

Every Sunday morning Granny Aẋu was up early with everyone else. Today was the day all the children went to Sunday school while the adults; pre-teens and teens attended the Anglican Church for service.

I was still in the Sunday school age group and we all went to the Parish Hall, which was between the Minister's home and the Anglican Church. Mom made sure that we wore our Sunday best. The men wore their Sunday dress clothes and the women wore their best dresses. Men and women always wore some type of hat on their heads. Everyone walked together from the Big House to the Church, picking up more family along the way who didn't reside in the Big House. The Church was only a five-minute walk away. If it were still berry picking time, some of the boys would race ahead and pick blackberries that were just off the beach while waiting for everyone else to catch up. Because I was a girl, Mom wouldn't let me go with them as much as I wanted to. I was wearing a dress and had to act like a little lady. She said, "You will get blackberry stains onto your dress or jacket so quit being a tomboy, walk like a lady should."

Once everyone reached the front of the church, we divided up into two groups with parents admonishing us to behave and listen to our Sunday school teacher, Frances Speck.

We started up the short hill to the Parish Hall as the older family marched in twos into the church. As we walked up the stairs to enter the Hall, organ music could be heard, played by Mrs. Kenmuir who was already inside the Church.

There was more than one Sunday school teacher and we were separated into certain age groups in the building. We quietly sat around while Mrs. Speck read us parts of the bible. After she was finished, sheets of paper were handed out to everyone then one child was designated to hand out crayons. The pictures that we colored always had something to do with the reading lesson given earlier. On this particular Sunday, I was given the one that was a picture of David walking with staff in hand across a pasture with his colorful jacket on and had sheep grazing in the background. This was one of the parts of Sunday school that we all enjoyed because we could talk out loud while coloring. Usually our talks centered on the lesson Mrs. Speck had read to us. The pictures always depicted some part of the story we had just heard.

The church was so close that the singers could be heard singing, in perfect harmony, the songs listed on the minister's small Hymn board at the front of the church. The best part was when the hymns were sung in kwak̓wala because there still were a lot of elders who knew how to sing in kwak̓wala. It seemed like the songs moved up a notch or two in volume. It was very peaceful and soothing listening to the singers and the organ music as they gave everything they had to the songs.

After the coloring sessions, the Sunday school teachers had everyone move the benches back into rows and we all congregated in one area. It was time for us to sing songs before Sunday school ended for the morning. We also enjoyed this and our favorites were "Jesus Loves Me" and "Deep and Wide." I often wondered if our elders enjoyed hearing us sing out in our immature voices while being led by the Sunday school teachers. I am quite sure that they could hear us between their hymns when the minister was reading passages from the Bible and reciting his sermon for the day.

Sunday school ended and we all went outside to wait for our parents who were still in the Church. We laughed and talked with cousins who didn't live in the Big House and other kids from the reserve. The boys climbed the cherry trees while waiting and I was jealous. I couldn't play with them because of the dress I was wearing.

The Church service usually ended five or ten minutes after Sunday school. We impatiently waited outside the church yard while the minister shook hands with his congregation as they filed by and he thanked them for attending the service.

This is the part that I didn't like as Granny Pearlie and others said, "Honey, you look nice today, you should wear dresses like that all the time" or something along those lines. I was worried that Mom might do just that and I dreaded having to wear dresses and having my hair put up in ponytails or pig tails. I preferred jeans and a t-shirt with some sort of headband to keep my hair out of my face.

I was anxious to reach the Big House so that I could put my "play clothes" back on before lunch. After we had eaten, Joe and I went looking for Phillip boy then walked over to Auntie Lena's to get Harry boy.

We sat on the swings in front of Auntie Lena's house trying to come up with something to do for the afternoon. We came to a consensus and we traipsed to the back of the Big House. There were plum trees right behind our house and I don't know if it belonged to Uncle Ben or Grampa Moses but everyone had the right to pick from them if they had the energy to climb the trees.

We all climbed the trees to get the best plums possible. Joe spotted this really prime looking plum and since Harry boy was the smallest and lightest out of all of us, he was chosen to go and get it.

With great agility, he climbed the biggest plum tree behind the house and started inching his way out on the branch. The rest of us were watching him as he shimmied along much like a caterpillar. He had both feet wrapped on the branch and was pulling himself along with his hands while lying on his belly. He reached the half way point on the branch and was almost to the plum that had our mouths watering in anticipation of that first bite. All of a sudden, we heard a cracking sound that we all recognized since we had all fallen out of trees at least once in our lives. Harry let out a loud yell then said, "Help me you guys! Highball, Highball!"

The branch hadn't completely snapped yet and his feet were dangling about ten feet from the ground. Harry was only gripping on with his hands. It wouldn't be much longer before the branch broke right off and Harry's descent would be fast and painful.

We looked below him and saw that there was a very large patch of dzandzanxtłam (stinging nettles) all around him. Harry looked down and saw his predicament and said, "Hurry and get sticks or something to knock them down before I fall in." There was genuine fright in his face as he realized he was only wearing sneakers and blue jean shorts.

All three of us raced into the house! We went to grab the broom and hockey sticks. Once we were back outside, we formed a straight line just far enough apart so that the flying nettles wouldn't sting us while we chopped away at them, working our way to where Harry was hanging on the tree.

It was slow work because these stinging nettles were at least five to six feet high! As we worked up a sweat swinging and clearing a trail, Harry never quit screaming at us to hurry up. Every so often we would hear another snap or crackling sound, which meant that the branch was on its last legs, and it made Harry holler even louder at us.

We were within two feet of Harry when the branch let go and he landed with a thud. He jumped up and ran out of there so fast, it looked like someone lit a match underneath him. He immediately broke out with huge red welts on every exposed part of his body from the stinging nettles. He was trying his best not to scratch but that was impossible.

Phillip boy said, "Someone said rubbing butter helps when you get stung." I ran into the Big House and grabbed a container of butter and all of us scooped a handful each then began massaging it all over Harry.

He was still in agony and Joe said, "Granny A̱xu said that ƚandak̲w (snot) is also good." Phillip boy and I looked at each other in disbelief as Harry told us to go ahead and do it. I thought he must be in a really lot of pain to allow us to do such a disgusting thing.

For some reason that I will never understand, we actually did it. Maybe it was some sort of revenge for all the times Harry and Dad had beat us in soccer or maybe we really believed it worked. Joe said that Granny believed it did or so Joe alleged and maybe that's why we were so willing to do it.

Harry finally quit scratching his body sometime after dinner but he ended up with small scratch marks that lasted for quite a few weeks. Once the itching phase disappeared, all of us laughed about what had happened including Harry. He could not fathom why he had let us rub his body with greasy butter and the other revolting substance. Oh, by the way, we never did get that plum which led to Harry's unfortunate accident.

Later on, Joe and I were playing with our sister when we accidentally hurt her. As she was the youngest of the three of us, Cory played her trump card and went squealing to our Dad as usual. She put on her best fake tears and we tried to explain what happened, which fell on deaf ears. We were told, "You both should know better. She is way smaller and you should go easy on her. Let her play with you guys and get along."

Granny had an elderly friend named Tsamaga who was now living in the Big House and Joe decided to get his revenge on Cory for being a tattle-tale. Tsamaga loved kids and always wanted Cory to sleep with her so Joe started to call Cory Tsamaga.

Joe said, "You better listen to us and quit telling on us or we'll go tell Tsamaga that you want to sleep with her tonight. You are just a big baby."

This always made Cory toe the line and if she really irritated Joe, he relentlessly called her by the nickname he had given her. It never failed to make her upset and she ended up snapping her eyes at him and storming out of the room. Cory's nickname stuck with everyone in the family and the name eventually changed to Charming Girl.

This particular Sunday night was one that we had been waiting impatiently for what seemed like forever. Our parents had said we could stay up late to watch "The Ed Sullivan Show" because the Beatles were appearing for the first time ever! Everyone in the Big House was coming to watch television with us that night.

To make things even better, the Canadian comedy act of "Wayne and Shuster" was on first. Parents and children loved to watch their slapstick antics. Looking back, I realize that our elders liked them because the actors weren't afraid to make fun of elected government officials and the policies they enacted that affected us. Most of kids liked them because they were just plain funny.

It was finally time for "The Ed Sullivan Show." Gundy and a zillion other teenaged girls were talking non-stop about the singing group that had us sitting on the edge of our seats for them to appear on our black and white television set.

Even I was not impressed with the trapeze acts from China that usually made me think that I would be able to do such death defying stunts when I grew up. I think this was because I wanted to see why the Beatles had my teenage cousins in a frenzy.

The moment finally arrived with Ed Sullivan introducing the mop haired boys from England. Gundy, Eva, Toomuch and others started to sing along with the songs they had heard on the radio. Some of them actually let out small screams and this totally amazed me.

Dad started to make fun of them and the teenagers rushed to the Beatles' defense immediately. The boys of the Big House were even impressed with the group. I guess this is when the boys started to dress in black clothing and turtleneck shirts whenever they went to Council Hall dances.

The Beatles came back on for an encore much to the joy of almost everyone sitting around our little apartment. Time flew by much too quickly for us. The next thing you know, the little hand puppet Toe Poe Gee Joe was saying, "Kiss me Goodnight, Eddie." Ed Sullivan kissed him goodnight then did his well renowned goodbye wave to the television cameras and his millions of fans.

Phillip boy, Joe and I begged Dad to watch "Bonanza" next and the familiar phrases were said "Go and ask your mothers, it's up to them." We ran to ask Auntie Eddie and Mom. We pulled the normal stunt that we used anytime we wanted to pull the wool over their eyes. We told them, "Dad and Uncle Phil said we could watch Bonanza if you say it is okay."

We were practically on our hands and knees saying, "Please let us, we know it's a school night but we probably will lie there talking about the Beatles all night. Let us watch Bonanza and we all promise to go right to sleep after that."

Permission was granted with the stipulation that we did not fool around and talk when sent to bed after Bonanza ended. We all loved watching Bonanza and that only occurred if the following Monday was a holiday or it was summertime.

Even with such limited nights of watching the program, we knew the cook Hop Sing, Little Joe and the rest of his family like they lived next door. After an action packed hour, the theme music for Bonanza came on and this signaled that the show was over for another week.

We all followed through with our promise of behaving and went right to bed but with a hidden agenda in mind. We were hoping that if we behaved, maybe it would become a Sunday night occurrence to watch Bonanza.

Chapter 20 - Competitions and Other Lessons

I forgot an earlier story about Uncle Charley-horse's family. Before Auntie Annie had married my dad's brother, she was in a tuberculosis hospital in Nanaimo for many years while still quite young. Auntie Annie-horse was always in and out of the hospital because of her illness after she had given birth to our cousins. This is why Oxley, Marianne and Toomuch are mentioned as part of the extended Big House family that I remember when growing up. Gramps and Granny more or less raised them until they were almost teenagers.

Toomuch was hired one afternoon to babysit for almost all the younger kids in the Big House. One day we were being a bit too hard to handle for so she came up with an idea. She called us all outside and said, "Let's have a race to see who is the fastest out of all of you." Toomuch was a very fast learner and had decided to copy one of Dad's tactics for keeping us out of mischief. The trick was to keep everything we did a competition and no one would ever back out.

There must have been at least fifteen of us at the starting line. Other cousins asked what we were doing and quickly joined. Toomuch explained the rules to us. We had to all start in front of the Big House, then to run to the Royal Café and back. The total distance was well over a mile!

It started out looking like a marathon because we were so closely packed at the start line. The smaller kids slowly dropped out and walked most of the way, then waited for the older ones by St Georges Hospital. Lavina, Tidi, Toomuch and others were still giving it all they had to the Royal Café. At the turn around spot, there were about ten left who were determined to win this race.

As soon as the smaller kids could see the older cousins in the distance, they started running back towards the rez and the Big House. As we all reached the beginning of the old B.C. Packers cannery, we realized that we were in the last two hundred meters or so. I was beginning to wither and only wanted to finish the race without giving up!

The family trait of always trying to do your best kicked me into maximum overdrive and I was able to keep up with the top ten runners until the last 100 meters.

One by one, the runners were left behind by the leaders. I felt disappointment that I wouldn't win Toomuch's race and achingly jogged the last little bit finishing in the top fifteen. I watched Toomuch and Harold finish first and second from some distance.

Both of them collapsed on the side of the road and congratulated each other and watched the rest of us finish the race. Everyone of the racers finished the race even though first and last were separated by at least three or four minutes.

We all felt a sense of accomplishment but Toomuch wasn't done yet. It was time for a game of Indian baseball (come hell or high water, she was determined to wear us out so that we could not terrorize the Big House when she was on duty).

Most of the parents came home after our game and our conniving babysitter had kept us out of the house all day so she didn't have to clean up after us. Toomuch still had to sit for us upstairs though. Mom and Dad had a bowling banquet to go to at the Royal Canadian Legion that night.

We went to our suite then she told us to sit down and watch television. Our cousin then said, "I am going into the kitchen to prepare my favorite pasta and meat sauce for us." We all knew that this really meant we were dining on Kraft Dinner and canned meatballs that evening.

After the dishes were done, we watched some of our favorite comedies on television. Because Cory was younger then Joe and I, she was sent to bed earlier. We liked being able to stay up a bit longer but then we remembered! Joe said "Oh, oh. We are in for it again" with dread in his voice.

Toomuch never failed to make us practice the "Jive"

and the "Twist" with her. Joe went first, then she grabbed me before the next song started. She pushed, pulled and twirled us around every time it was our turn to dance. It felt like my arm sockets were pulling apart each time I was spun around. At first the spinning was fun because it made us dizzy but soon it started to give us a headache.

Joe actually gave me a sorrowful look when Toomuch sent him to bed because he knew that my lessons were not over yet. I was never so grateful in all my life when my bedtime curfew rolled around. I'm not saying Joe and I didn't love Toomuch but this is one of the reasons that her nickname was just TOO MUCH!

I slowly walked to bed and was bent over with every muscle hurting in my body. It took forever to get my pajamas on. It was such a relief to crawl between the sheets. It must have been sometime after eleven when I woke up and had to go use the washroom downstairs.

Just before I went down the stairs, I noticed one of my parent's friends at the bottom of the stairs. Martha Peterson was removing her shoes ever so quietly then she tiptoed by the door that went into the living room so Granny Axu wouldn't see her. I watched her carry her shoes and daintily run the first few steps. I quickly stepped back into the shadows of one of the rooms and watched her go into our apartment.

I woke Joe up and watched a few more adults repeat the same thing. We watched puzzled, then we stealthily went into Mom and Dad's bedroom using a passkey that they hid outside their door (they did not know we knew about the key). This let us sneak back into our apartment unnoticed to see what the big secret was.

We saw that it was Alfred and Lorraine Cook, along with Martha's husband Gordie, members of the bowling league who had ran up the stairs. Joe and I looked at each other when we recognized the sound of the old pulley system creaking away that hung just outside our kitchen window. The pulley system was a big Coca-Cola box on rollers that used to carry wood up from the ground floor. Dad built it for us so we wouldn't have to walk the two flights of stairs with heavy loads of firewood. We both knew it was no longer used since we were on oil now and wondered why on earth they would be using the old system and so late at night.

Our questions were answered very quickly when the familiar sound of bottles clinking was heard. Our parents were sneaking a couple of cases of beer past Granny Axu to celebrate winning the bowling league!

We kept peeking out the curtain that was the door to our parents' bedroom throughout the night. The music started out nice and low while they discussed bowling then it slowly inched up in volume.

I finally saw how people who grew up doing the dances when they were teenagers did the "Jive" and the "Twist." I looked at Joe, rolled my eyes and said "It looks like we are going to be dancing with Toomuch for a few more nights unless Mom gets us another sitter. She still can't dance like that with us yet."

It was really something to see our parent let loose and have fun with their friends and family. This was the first time that we had seen them dance. The men were working up a sweat while dancing to the old records and the women were very good dancers. We were very surprised that Granny never came up the stairs to tell them to quit jumping on the third floor and making her living room light sway around downstairs.

I finally fell asleep but with King Richard singing Honey, Honey, Honey, Tutti Fruitti and Let's Twist Again as my lullabies that night. The songs eventually worked their way into my dreams that night.

I woke up the next morning wondering if my parents really thought they fooled Granny A̱xu. Joe and I talked it over and decided it was much like my times table blackboard. Granny decided to let our parents get away with it this time but to this day we don't know why.

Chapter 21 - Hairy Days Ahead

It came to be that time of year that all the boys in the family did not look forward to. I saw Phillip boy and Lee head down the stairs with tears running down their faces. As they walked, they pleaded with Auntie Eddie who was in front of them. Both of them kept saying, "Please Mom, no one cuts their hair like that anymore!"

I realized then that it was time to go to see Uncle Dayu. The boys lined up like ducks in a shooting gallery. Uncle pulled out the old buzz cut razor. He plugged it in and I saw every one of my cousins wince like they had been slapped. Phillip boy had confided in me that the sound of that razor struck terror in his heart much like the sound of a dentist's drill.

Uncle didn't just trim the boys' hair. He left each and every one of them with a cue ball head. Uncle Dayu did his only son's cut first then the oldest nephew went next until he had sheared every one of them and there was enough hair on the floor to stuff a pillowcase. It never failed; the first one off the barber chair rubbed the top of his head and felt nothing but nubs. They looked in the bathroom mirror and I never understood why because the haircuts were exactly the same each time they had it cut. Maybe they were hoping Uncle showed a bit of mercy on this particular day and left just a little at the back or at the sides of the head.

Another time Dad bought new hair cutting shears and he offered to cut Uncle Ass's hair since Uncle Dayu was out of town. Needless to say, Uncle was a bit leery with good reason to be. Dad sat him on one of our kitchen chairs upstairs and wrapped a ripped garbage bag around his shoulders.

We were sitting in the living room when we heard him start up the shears. This looked like it would be fun to watch so we moved into the kitchen to watch. Dad immediately went straight up the back of his head at full speed.

"What are you doing Joe?!" Uncle Ass asked my Dad. His voice already sounded like he was having second thoughts in trusting my father.

Dad said, "It's okay, I'm just making the mark to show how short I am going to cut it." Meanwhile he had this big smirk on his face and was trying not to laugh out loud. He continued on with what was supposed to be a trim, but it was starting to look like the haircuts that the boys had recently received.

There was one problem though. Dad did not have the deftness and the eyeball to make it just right like Uncle Dayu could.

He could not hold his laugh in any longer and Uncle was really getting worried now. Dad kept saying it looks all right but every one of us could see that his hair looked awful. The harder Dad laughed, the angrier Uncle became.

Uncle Ass finally ended up getting off the chair to end his torture at the hands of my Dad. He went to look in the mirror and immediately put a baseball cap on. His hair was poking out in small porcupine patches all over his head with uneven lengths. Dad just kept smiling and saying, "It will grow back in. Your hair doesn't look that look that bad Ass." Uncle just stormed out of the apartment wearing that old baseball cap and we never saw him without it for the next three months.

I'm not trying to say that the boys had it harder than us because our family had a different type of hair torture for the girls in the family. Auntie Lena was our hairdresser and it was no Sunday picnic either.

Mom would march me over to Auntie Lena's house with an old worn out sheet in hand. I sat there in her chair and it was my turn to almost be in tears. My Mom and Auntie ripped the sheet into strips until they were almost the same length while I watched them with dread.

Auntie tipped me over her sink and made sure my hair was wet. She used a towel to lightly dry it. I then had to sit on one of her kitchen chairs while she grabbed small sections of my long hair. She then proceeded to wrap them much like you see them do to mummies at the movies. It usually took over three hours of sitting there and I was in excruciating pain thinking of how she was only up to the first set of twenty strips of hair wrapping. I still had another sixty or seventy more to go!

After every strand of hair was bound tightly in the pieces of sheet, I then had to walk home like that in front of all my friends and leave them in overnight. I was a tomboy and this was a punishment worse then being grounded in my mind. The only thing that made me feel better was that I wouldn't be the only one looking like this for a full day. We passed Tidi as she was heading to Auntie Lena's with her mother. I knew that Auntie Lena was going to give Tidi and Lavina more of the same treatment so I knew that the three of us would be suffering together.

The next morning Mom removed the strips of cloth and made me look in a mirror. To my horror, I thought I looked like a darker version of Shirley Temple and probably would've looked like the black dancing partner's daughter if he had one in the movie "The Good Ship Lollipop" that we had just seen in the Bay Theatre.

I was so grateful that the curliness only lasted for two or three days. I swear that I would've even beaten up my favorite cousin Phillip boy if I had to endure one more day of his teasing and whistling at me. It was bad enough Joe and I were mocking each other constantly and we actually did end up wrestling around, inflicting physical pain on each other.

Chapter 22 - Fun and Games

Once our hair went back to normal, we started to play outside again. A new refrigerator was bought for the Big House. The huge cardboard box it came in was pulled up and over the fridge then thrown out the back porch.

We happened to stumble across it and brought it over past Uncle Ben's house where there was a small hill. The box fit five of us into it and we played war games and we used it as a bunker until we tired of shooting each other. As we sat around on the grassy knoll, we tried to think of what we could use the box for next.

Phillip boy said "Let's all get inside and roll it down this hill." It sounded like fun and we all crawled into it. On the count of three, we all did a roll inside and kept this up until we reached the bottom of the small hill. It made us slightly dizzy so we kept doing it over and over.

This still wasn't entertaining and challenging enough so Lavina said "Why don't we go down the hill and through the blackberry bushes until we reach the road." This sounded like more of a challenge so off we went to the top of the hill again.

We took more of a running start and tried to gain momentum before we bulldozed our way into four-foot high blackberry bushes. We started off really well then we started to tire. The thorns on the bushes were hooking and slowing us down.

I happened to be on of one side of the box and tried to peek out to see how far we were. All I received for my efforts was a scratch on my forehead from a prickle. We looked at each other and realized that we might have a bit more than we could chew this time. Joe said that he hoped we didn't run over a bunch of snakes and I was petrified of the slinky, scaley creatures. This gave Lavina and I incentive to start to rant at the boys to get into battle speed, just like Charlton Heston had in the movie "Ben Hur".

It took us twenty minutes of hard somersaults inside that box to get where we knew we were almost out of blackberry bushes. We could hear cars close by. After a short break, everyone counted out, " One, two, three," and we burst out of the blackberry bushes. We came out too fast and could not stop our forward momentum. We hurtled across the road, over the seawall and onto the beach.

That might've hurt us but wouldn't you know our luck, it was late fall, the time of big tides and it was high water. We started pushing and shoving each other as we went splat into the cold water. This was one time that we really were in over our heads and knew it.

We started swimming toward the seawall that ran beside the road. Once Lavina was able to get a good grip, she climbed up and out of the water. Lavina reached down and pulled us out one by one. Now we had to try and sneak back into the house without getting caught. We knew that we would be in a lot of trouble for falling into the ocean.

The best thing we could think of was to run and hide in the basement until a plan came to one of us. Shivering away, we huddled around the furnace all talking at once. One plan was to stay in the basement and let the furnace dry us off. That proved to be impractical as our lips were turning blue and how would we explain the salt all over our faces and arms.

We decided that a scout would be sent ahead to see if the coast was clear in the kitchen. If it was, we would borrow clothing off the clothesline and the girls would sprint to the washroom to change first. Once they finished, they would distract anyone that might come by and the boys would do the same thing.

Our wet clothing was thrown into the laundry piles and we all went to our proper rooms to put our own stuff on. After that was completed the borrowed things were placed back onto the lines.

We all met back in the basement to talk about what happened and realized that we just saved ourselves from some real punishment this time. At first we laughed about it and thought it was funny until Harry boy finally made us realize how reckless we had been when he said "We were lucky that no car passed by and ran us over when we came out of the bushes."

Then it hit us that it was lucky that we all knew how to swim. What if we had someone with us who didn't know how to swim? Would we have been able to save them if it came to that?

It scared us when we realized that we were pushing our luck way too much, trying to create new ways to have fun. I think that was one of the days we said that we really would put more thought into what we did but deep down I didn't know if we could.

Chapter 23 - Sports Day

Our small town always celebrated Queen Victoria Day (May Day) with the municipality. May Day weekend and our Annual Native June Sports were two of the special times that we were bought new clothes by our parents.

Native people came in from all the surrounding villages because these celebrations had races, parades, soccer tournaments and dances that everyone participated in (during the June Sports weekend, there were also usually one or two potlatches).

The living room in the Big House was always packed with families from neighboring villages. Both of the couches turned into double beds and children slept on the floor in sleeping bags. We usually gave up our beds and couches in our small apartment for Auntie Dianna's family who came up from Vancouver.

Granny A̱xu always had the kids march in the parade in full regalia. I remember one outfit that she made for George. He was dressed in cedar bark from head to toe.

She had made a cedar bark headpiece, vest, Hamat'sa skirt, wrist and ankle bracelets. George looked awesome and proud walking down the street in his cedar bark regalia. The rest of the family walked along with him in their colorful button blankets and aprons.

Once the parade reached the soccer field, the preacher had a small church service to bless the salmon fleet (when our town used to have a fleet). Some kwak'wala songs were sung and a dance was performed. Prizes were given out and George won First Prize for his cedar bark outfit.

After that, we all went home to put on our new clothes and raced back for the track and field events that were held for all ages. The events included the high jump, long jump and relays. The Sports Committee tried to have something for everyone so there were also fun events like the watermelon, cracker and potato races for kids and adults. There was a slow bike race, baby bottle race and a greasy pole event. Every event had a first, second and third place ribbon with a small cash prize for weekend spending money.

In the slow bike race, one had to try to be the last to get across the finish line. The hardest part that we found was not to touch the ground or hit another bike. As soon as you fell over or touched the ground, you were eliminated. Everyone zigged and zagged trying to be the last across the line.

The baby bottle race was exactly that. A bottle was

filled with soft drinks and you had to suck it until the bottle was finished. To further complicate it, a partner had to pack you on their knees. You were allowed to trade places but once the bottle was finished, you had to burp then race fifty yards across a finish line. Some of the more adventurous elders removed their false teeth to try and gain an edge for faster gum suction. They looked very funny talking and laughing during the race.

The greasy pole was smothered in lard and was about ten feet high. On top of the pole, an envelope was tacked with a fifty-dollar bill inside. All you were given were a pair of overalls that was shared by everyone who wished to attempt to get the money on the top of the pole.

There was always a line up because fifty dollars was a lot of money at the time. Some people would almost reach the top then the grease became too slippery to keep a good grip and they slid back down in frustration. Kids had to roll the arms and legs up because it was a one size must fit all outfit.

The overalls were eventually covered in grease and became harder and harder to use. Kids and adults alike rolled around in the dirt to try and get further up the pole but the greasy pole usually lasted for most of the day. These three races always created excitement, with much laughter by the contestants and fans watching.

Soccer games started in the afternoon. There were a couple of ladies teams, lots of kids teams and adult men teams from surrounding villages. Our field was nothing to brag about. It was all dirt with many pebbles everywhere. Teams were covered in mud when it rained and covered in dust if it was hot. At times, the volunteer fire department had to come and hose the field down because it was so dusty. Players and fans both couldn't find the ball during these times.

If there happened to be a potlatch going on, we could all hear the singers beating the hollow log and drums and singing the mourning songs. I will never forget running around playing soccer and hearing the beat echoing around the reserve. It seemed fitting because it was our native June Sports Event.

During the evening, everyone went to the Big House for the potlatch. The Grand Finale occurred on Sunday when the soccer teams in the finals went at it head to head.

The women's final was first and it set the stage for the men's final. The two women's teams were Alert Bay Cormorettes and the Kingcome Wolverines. Both the teams were named after well-established men's soccer clubs.

Villages loved their teams and it was always intense, with fans from both sides cheering until they were hoarse. Fans stayed on opposite sides of the field because it could get down right nasty if you happened to be standing amongst the wrong fans that were cheering for the other team. It didn't matter if you had family on the other team; loyalties were strong for the hometown that you happened to live in. The amazing thing was that this was the women's final and we hadn't even had the kick off for the Men's Championship game yet.

The men's final usually came down to the Kingcome Wolves versus the Alert Bay Cormorants and this year was no different.

The players played with a passion and skill that is still talked about to this day. The title meant everything to the winning team because it gave them bragging rights until the next year and no one liked to be on the losing side.

I can't recall who won because the title changed hands so many times between the two teams. They were so evenly matched in skill, heart and determination that the final game could go either way any given year. All I know is that those players have passed on the same soccer drive to many generations of kwaḵwala speaking people.

Chapter 24 - Religious Doubts

I was home upstairs in the Big House one school day all by myself but I seem to recall other people being downstairs. Mom had kept me home because I had a bad chest cold. I was lying down reading comic books and magazines that Dad had bought to keep me quiet. If I had nothing to read, there was no way that I would stay in bed throughout the day with no adult supervision.

After taking my morning cough syrup and reading for a bit, I dozed off to sleep. I awoke to a loud bang that sounded like a car backfiring. I sleepily walked over to the window by the Dick girls' bedroom since that is where the noise originated.

I saw no car and nothing out of the ordinary whatsoever so I went back to bed. After twenty minutes or so I heard the ambulance siren, which sounds different from a fire alarm, I then knew that it was no car backfiring that I had heard earlier. I hated the sounds of fire trucks and ambulances especially since they seemed to always be coming onto the reserve.

I silently wished for the wail of the siren to fade off into the distance for that would mean it was heading to the municipality side of town. Deep down inside I knew that it was going to head my way because of the loud bang that went off earlier.

No one ever wanted to hear any type of sirens in our small town because it never seemed to bring good news to anyone. I was right and the ambulance siren became louder and louder. I looked out our living room window upstairs, which faced the main road, and saw the ambulance in front of Mrs. Cranmer's.

It slowed down and made a turn up the side of the Big House to the driveway that led to my Great-Uncle Ben's House. I left the apartment and went to the window at that side of the house, dreading what I would see.

I opened the window and looked out. The ambulance workers were pulling a gurney out the back of the ambulance and they went into Great-Uncle Ben's house. Something made me stand there and watch even though I didn't want to.

After what seemed like hours, they came out with someone strapped down and placed onto the gurney. They carefully carried the gurney out the front door and down the stairs towards the ambulance.

That's when I noticed that the sheet went completely over the person's head. It hit me then that this person was dead and it was going to be another family member. I saw my cousin Barb Alfred being hugged and consoled by an older person but I didn't know who it was. I think my mind purposely blanked certain sections out to save me pain and grief. I am not even sure if it was Barb or I just thought it was because she lived there.

Numb, I closed the window and went back to bed because I knew that family would start to arrive at the Big House quickly once the word had spread around the reserve. Many relatives did come in and out of the house throughout the day. I felt sick to my stomach, which had nothing to do with my cold.

I tried reading but had to keep going back to the same chapter. I could not retain what my brain was seeing or make any sense of the words and sentences. My thoughts kept going back to my brother Joe because he always went to visit "his" Uncle Ben if he had a chance. I hoped that it wasn't Great-Uncle Ben that they had carried out of the house. I was so afraid of what I would find out that I didn't eavesdrop on our elders as they were speaking. Something I usually did whenever I wanted to know what was happening.

Joe came home and told me that everyone at school was saying that Uncle Ben had shot himself. He asked me if it was true and I said, "I don't know. I was too scared to go and ask. I didn't go downstairs at all today."

He went straight to Dad and asked if it was true. Dad said, "Yes, he had cancer and the pain became too much for him to take anymore." I don't know if this was the truth or if this was Dad's way of trying to make it easier for us to deal with.

This is when I began to doubt the good works of God. I wondered why people that were close to us and had done no wrong had to die. Why did they become so sick that the pain was unbearable, why did young cousins die in house fires, why did Auntie Annie spend so much time in the hospital?

All these thoughts and many others ran through my head. I went to look at that big Bible I loved to read and it gave me no quick answers. I put the book down in frustration. Looking around the house, I couldn't fathom how my elders were able to hang onto their beliefs in a loving God. They were able to grasp something that made them so devoted to the teachings of the Bible that I still could not understand.

All I could do was hope that I would one day be able to find the elusive anwers they had found that would help me deal with this terrible hurt inside.

Chapter 25 - Imaginations

The family sent us to the movies one Saturday afternoon and it was a John Wayne western. We came home all hyped up and dug around for old cowboy hats that the boys received for Christmas presents. Phillip boy went to strip some alder branches of its leaves to make a bow. We borrowed some leftover wool from Granny A<u>x</u>u to make the rest of the bow.

Our imaginations took over and we made the arrows that we would be shooting. The six-shooters were our fingers. The two banister railings on the second floor became our horses. Pillows were adapted to become our saddles and large towels magically turned into the western blankets we saw on the horses at the movies.

My brother Joe's old horse on springs was what our fearless leader rode. The Big House rang out with the bugle call blown by Joe since he owned the lead horse. Indian War cries bounced off the walls as we tried to stem off the attacking bluecoats.

Most of the time, we wanted to be cowboys or part of

the American Army because we had been so brainwashed into not wanting to be native. Another reason was because in every movie we ever saw the Indians never won a battle. Battle cries, agonized death throes and calls for help went on for the rest of the afternoon.

Once we tired of this, we decided to play hide and seek downstairs. We did the eennie, meenie, miny, moe rhyme to see who had to count first. Home base was placed into the kitchen so that we wouldn't accidentally hit Granny as we tore around the corner into the long hallway.

She just sat there and watched us sprint by as we raced to get to the base whenever we were caught. We ended getting too boisterous and were finally asked to go and play outside.

As we sat around outside talking, I finally noticed that Phillip boy wasn't with us. I asked where he was and then remembered! He had asked me to hang him up on one of the coat racks in the long hallway and put an overcoat over him. I had left him standing on a three-inch ledge four feet off the ground.

We went back in and he was squirming around trying to get himself off the rack. He had thrown off the overcoat but was unable to lift himself up high enough to remove his collar from the hanger. All he said to us was, "Get me down. I thought you guys were just kidding me when you all went outside. I didn't know that you forgot all about me."

He thought it was a good hiding spot. It certainly proved to be since no one found him and we had all forgotten about him.

We went into the basement to play on the tire swing that was there and someone suggested that we take it down. After taking it down we removed the rope and Harry boy said, "Now what do we do with it?"

Harold said, "Let's crawl inside and take turns rolling down the hill beside the house." I thought to myself that once again we were doing something that we hadn't really put much deliberation into and the possible consequences that could occur. I was too scared to voice what I was thinking out loud because then the rest of the gang would say I was jamming out.

I did have the brains enough to not volunteer to go first; Phillip boy was more then willing to do that. We carried the wheel outside and rolled the tire up the hill. Phillip boy crawled into the tire and looked like a caterpillar that was trying to inch its way along an alder branch.

He had his feet on a funny angle trying to maintain a good grip. His hands were contorted and twisted as he tried to keep from falling out of the tire. Harry boy ran to the bottom of the hill to make sure that no cars were coming from either direction. Once he yelled out that it was okay, two or three of the boys started running with Phillip boy to help him gain momentum.

We could hear him laughing as his speed picked up and we ran along with him as he rolled down the hill. I thought that he would topple over eventually but he made it to the bottom of the hill.

He passed Harry boy by the side of the road and rolled over a small stoop and carried on down a small porch of a house that was built on pilings on the beach. There was a loud bang as he hit the door that led into the kitchen of the house. The next thing we knew, he was inside that house!

Phillip boy crawled out of the tire and staggered around. The rolling motion had made him very dizzy and the person who lived in the house was giving him absolute heck. She threw our tire down the beach and Phillip boy was running and apologizing as he was being yelled at.

It was decided that the tire would go back onto the rafters and remain a swing. We would keep these types of adventures for the next time we went to Vancouver to the PNE where the "Spider" and "Monster Mouse" rides were run by trained technicians.

Chapter 26 - Womanhood Strikes

I went to see my Mom and asked her what was going on. I was scared because I was bleeding and she explained that this was a woman's curse in life. She showed me how to use all the gadgets and how to attach the necessary parts to be workable. It felt like I was wearing a shin guard between my legs.

I found this terribly disgusting and once again wished I had been born a boy. I didn't like the cramps and the zits breaking out on my face that came with my new womanhood. I understood why Mom said it was a curse. I hated the cutesy little sayings like "My friend is visiting right now" that stopped me from swimming with the rest of the gang.

It even interfered with my fun times with Phillip boy. Phillip boy's Dad gave us money to spend at Cranmer's Pool Hall. We were out bike riding and I was double riding him as we headed to the candy store to buy gum and drinks.

After carefully choosing our treats, we jumped back

onto the bike and I was double riding him past the Council Hall. Besides the curse, I was beginning to develop breasts and was very self-conscious of that fact.

We were using Phillip boy's bike and he was sitting on the crosspiece right in front of me. We picked up speed as we zoomed down the road. He reached back and tried to get a bubble gum out of my shirt pocket that just happened to be smack on one of my developing breasts.

I panicked and let one handlebar go and slapped his hand away. He was so surprised because I never had a problem when he reached into that same pocket in the past. He jerked back and this caused me to lose control of the bike.

We teetered and wobbled towards the seawall at the end of the apartments that used to belong to Grampa Moses. We were off balance and travelling quite fast. The front tire hit the seawall and we flipped upwards and onto the beach.

I landed on the small rocks on the beach with only some scratches from broken glass with the bike on top of me. I quickly threw the bike off me and went to see what had happened to Phillip boy.

He had landed on his stomach on one of the big logs that was tied up for firewood. He could hardly breathe because the wind had been knocked out of him. I'm pretty sure that he hit his head too because he wasn't making sense when I asked if he was okay. Phillip boy eventually came to his senses and asked why I had hit him so hard.

I said that I was just surprised but was too embarrassed to tell him the real reason. I still wanted to be
thought of as one of the boys. If I admitted that I was going through these changes, I stupidly thought I might be
excluded from playing with him and my other male cousins.

We then set to work on packing the bike back onto the
road. Both of us prayed that nothing happened to the bike
because it was an expensive item that we always had to
make sure we took care of. Money was not easy to come
by for our parents and our bikes were something that we
all treasured.

After a careful examination, the chain was the only
thing that came loose and that was easy to put back into
place. While Phillip boy was fixing the chain, Lavina came
to see if we were all right because she saw us going over the
seawall. I whispered to her and told her the real reason that
I had reacted to Phillip boy's harmless attempt to reach
for gum. She burst out laughing but did say that she was
glad that we never really got hurt and was happy that the
bike was still going to work.

We went to get Lavina's bike and decided to go and
race around the BC Packers Office. Lee, Joe and Georgie
boy decided to join us on our biking expedition. The goal
was to race around the building thirty times to see who
was the fastest. We bent our least favorite hockey cards
and put them in between the tire spokes to give us added
sound effects for the races. More kids joined us and by the

time we started the first race, there were over twenty bikes in a row at the start line.

One person was designated to yell, "Get set, GO!" and we were off. Bikes of all colors, sizes and name brands took off and were tightly packed for the first three turns around the building then the pack started to thin out. The click, click of the hockey cards could clearly be heard and that was the sound of a Harley-Davidson in our young minds. Everyone had to slow down a bit on the corners on the wharf area because the wood was still damp from the rain the night before.

I almost wiped out on one corner just before hitting the pavement and barely gained control before Georgie boy came barreling straight at me. He laughed as he saw the fear in my eyes as we barely avoided a major pile-up with the other racing bikes that were hot on his heels.

The other bikes whizzed by me and I was left near the end of the pack after gaining control. All I could do now was try to save face and not give up. There was no way that I was going to catch the leaders.

Lavina, Georgie boy and Phillip boy finished the race in that order. We all lined up to have another race because we all wanted a chance to say that we had won at least one race when catastrophe struck me and hard.

I was coming around the corner and Georgie boy yelled at me so I looked back. He said, "There is a car coming at you, Watch Out!"

I looked forwards and saw a car coming at me. I was

hit square on and landed on the hood of the car. I vaguely remember falling off and hitting the ground. I tried to stand up and go and check on my bike but couldn't put any weight on my left leg. I fell back onto the ground.

My front tire rim was bent almost in half and I knew that I wouldn't be riding that bike for quite awhile. The man who was driving the car came over to where I was sitting on the ground and asked if I was okay.

I told him that I couldn't stand on my left leg so he picked me up and put me into his car. I yelled at my brother, "Try and get my bike home okay."

While all this was going on Phillip boy had jumped on his bike and zoomed to the Big House to tell my Dad what had happened to me. We were almost to the Drugstore when my Dad caught up to us in his car. He honked his horn to get us to stop then he moved me over into his car but not after giving an earful to the person that had accidentally hit me.

Dad finished driving me to the hospital and carried me where Mom happened to be working that day. She casually placed me into a wheelchair, whereas my Dad was in a panic trying to see what was wrong with me. The two parents were quite the contrast. Dad had made me feel like crying because he was so upset and was scaring me. Mom was calm, cool and collected and quickly made me feel that everything was going to be okay.

Doctor Pickup came to look me over and gave me some painkillers. Dad sat there the whole time waiting to see what the verdict would be. Mom came in and said that I would have to stay overnight to make sure that I hadn't hurt my head or had any internal injuries.

Dad still looked furious and Mom told him to keep his temper when he went to find out how I had ended up getting hit by the car. He was very protective of each and every one of us in the family so there was a need for Mom to say that to him.

Mom and other nurses kept checking up on me for the next hour or so. The only thing that really hurt was my left knee and the few small scratches that I had received from the black topped road. I guess Doctor Pickup had told the nurses to make sure that I didn't go to sleep for a couple of hours in case of a concussion.

The gang all dropped by to visit and Georgie boy had his usual sly humor and comments about how I had looked flying over that car. Georgie boy said, "You looked like those guys on motorcycles that try to jump over ten cars but you didn't make it."

As usual, he had us all laughing because he made any serious situation comical. I told him I would have seen the car if he hadn't called me and made me look backwards, but he had a smart answer all ready for anything that I had to say, typical Georgie boy.

Dad came by with new comics and soft drinks for me to make the small hurts go away. I think that's why most of us didn't mind being sick or hurt because we were usually babied by others in the family. The nurses eventually told everyone that it was time to go because I needed to rest. After I had eaten dinner, I fell asleep only to awaken an hour or so later with a huge, swollen left knee that was throbbing intensely.

I was given crutches so that I could get to the washroom but it was too awkward so I ended up just jumping on one foot, much like hopscotch, to get to the can. Some patients started yelling at me to quit fooling around in the halls because the hopping had woken them up.

I tried to put weight on my left leg but almost collapsed as pain seared up into my knee. I ended up having to hop once again but tried my best to be quiet. After awkwardly crawling back into bed, I buzzed a nurse who came and gave me some painkillers so I could go to sleep that night.

I was woken up early the next morning, placed into a wheelchair and taken for x-rays. The doctor came by and said that nothing was broken but I would have to stay in for a couple of more days to see why I wasn't able to stand on my left leg. The novelty of being in the hospital was wearing thin and I was getting bored because no one could visit me until 3 o'clock. The swelling in my knee had gone down but I still couldn't put any weight onto it without it buckling under me.

Mom was working so she checked in on me every so often and Granny Pearlie came to say hi from the kitchen where she was the cook. These short visits broke up the monotony for me.

I was anxious when the doctor told Mom he was going to try something to get motion in my left knee. I really wanted to get out of the hospital but dreaded whatever procedure the doctor had in mind.

The doctor came in and froze my left leg then grabbed a huge needle after five minutes or so. I immediately looked away and held on tightly to my mom's hand. Mom said, "He is going to poke that needle into your knee and hit the nerves that aren't allowing you to step on your foot."

I probably didn't feel anything but broke into tears anyway because it made me feel better and that needle was huge in my eyes. I ended up crying myself to sleep and remember Mom telling me to quit being such a big baby. I thought to myself, let me put that needle into your knee and see how much you would like it.

The next morning I was able to walk short distances on my left leg and I think that deep down, I was trying extra hard because I didn't want to face those two needles once again.

Later that day; much to my relief, I was allowed to go home. Dad wheeled me to the door in that same wheelchair I came in on even though I was able to briefly walk on my own.

I was so happy to be going home and was walking better and better. Sports came first in my life and I would have been devastated if my tomboy career came to an abrupt end.

I was feeling better in no time because my brother and

I immediately got into a fight the first week I was home. He did something that really irritated me and I chased him up into the attic.

I tried to follow him up the stairs but my knee was still not strong enough to catch him yet. He was standing at the top in the shadows and daring me to come up after him. I called out, "You're dead Joe!"

I was about three steps into the enclosed stairwell and Joe tumbled a ten pin bowling pin down the steps aiming for me. I just jumped back in time before the pin nailed me on my shin. He laughed manically taunted me to try and come up the stairs, holding bowling pins in either hand. He had pulled a large bucket filled with bowling pins to the top of the stairs and had enough ammunition to last for quite some time.

Joe clipped me on the shin on the third or fourth pin and I felt pain much like when you hit your funny bone, which froze me for a split second. That frozen moment in time allowed Joe to hit me with a perfectly thrown bowling pin onto my still healing knee.

Every time I tried to go and get him, he rifled another pin at me and I had to run off to the side to dodge his artillery. It came down to a chess match. I had to try and make him use up his weapons so that I could start my full frontal assault. He'd taunt me and I'd yell back, "You're eventually going to run out, Joe, and then you'll be sorry!"

I knew that he didn't have that many pins left and

Joe was really going to get it from me when I finally reached him. The moment had arrived as I saw Joe looking right and left for something to throw down the stairs!

I put my head down and tore up the stairs. I reached the top and couldn't see Joe. The attic only had one small window and no lights whatsoever. It took me a few seconds for my eyes to adjust, as I looked right then left searching for that little bugger.

I heard a noise in one direction and started to head that way. The sneaky creep had thrown a boot to the left and sprinted down the stairs when I had cleared the path for him!

He was laughing because he thought he had escaped. Damn the pain in my knee, I pursued him down the steps as fast as humanly possible. Joe made the second set of stairs and I reached over the railing to try and grab his hair.

Cursing Uncle Dayu and his haircuts, Joe escaped my clutches by the skin of his bald head. Looking back at me laughing, Joe headed down the hallway and out towards the back door.

I knew that Joe would head to visit a cousin and he would use the trail behind the Big House to get there. He would want to gloat about how he had evaded my clutches.

I quickly grabbed a coke bottle and climbed out a window, which was now Joe's room. In my mind, this was a fitting way to get my revenge. He was walking by and I let loose with a perfect volley. The bottle glanced off of his shaved head and he looked up at me in shock.

Gone was that gloating look and the laughter. Once again, I realized too late what I had done and knew that I was in for it. Thank god, there was no blood and Joe had only received a glancing blow to the top of his hard head.

I climbed back into the house and ran to try and squeal on Joe about his instigation of the battle before the damage was done. At the same time, he was running back to the house to beat me to a parent and tell his version.

I was given supreme heck because I could have seriously hurt him with the coke bottle. Joe snickered under his breath. Then Dad turned to him and it was his turn as he said, "Honey's knee is still tender and you might have made it worse. Don't you two ever use your brains?"

The end result was that we were both grounded but I knew that more battles were ahead of us.

Chapter 27 - Life by the Water

My Dad used to work over at Telegraph Cove milling lumber. He used to go over with his friend, Gordon, who we all called "Box." They went across on Gramps' seine boat, the *Kiona*. It usually took them about half an hour to get across to the Cove.

It must have been some sort of holiday because I went across with my parents one time and slept on the boat with them. I was so excited to be going on the seine boat that most of our family had fished on at one time or another.

I ran down the dock but ended up waiting for my Dad to pack me across certain parts. We had to cross skinny little planks that joined the sections of the wharf together. I always remembered Lavina being stuck under those logs and I was afraid that I might end up trapped under the wharf if I fell off the planks.

Dad lifted me onto the *Kiona* then went back up the wharf to get the groceries that we would need while at Telegraph Cove. Mom told me to stay near her and said, "Don't be running around. There are a lot of things you

might trip over and you could end up falling overboard."
I found that amusing since Mom didn't even know how
to swim.

Dad and Box both came down with their arms loaded with groceries. I went and followed my Dad around
as he started the boat up. When the engine turned over,
I was surprised at how noisy it was. I peered down the
engine room but was a little afraid to go and look at what
was down there. Everything was a new experience for me
since I had never really been on a seiner before. I think I
was driving him crazy with all my questions but he answered every one of them.

Box climbed off the boat to let the lines go and he
looked pretty funny because he was even shorter than my
Dad. He had no problem jumping off the boat but getting
back on with his short legs was a totally different story.
He struggled to lift his legs onto the boat with his blue
overalls hanging past his runners. The straps kept dropping down over his shoulders as he finally made it onto
the deck.

I went to sit up top where Dad was holding the wheel
as we pulled out of the Bay. It felt so good to be sitting
beside him as we headed down Johnstone Strait. The
wind was blowing in my face but the sun kept me warm. I
looked up and saw the fishing company flag atop the mast,
fluttering in the ocean breeze.

We traveled so close to the beach when we rounded
Pepper's Point that I was able to clearly see my friend

Wendy's house.

There was so much to see that I didn't know where to look next. It was so much different than being on the *Island Princess* ferry that took us to Kelsey Bay. The *Kiona* traveled much closer to the shoreline of Vancouver Island. There were eagles soaring overhead and sitting on cedar trees along the rocky banks that we passed.

Dad pointed out a group of porpoises swimming by, which brought a big smile to my face. I fell in love with the boat at that moment and never wanted to get off!

Box yelled, "Look over there Joe, Jumpers!" I quickly turned to where he was pointing and saw nothing.

Dad explained to me, "Box just saw a sockeye jumping. Sockeye jump straight up in the air. Humpies jump out then kind of slide sideways then go back into the water. When we are out fishing, the skipper tries to catch the fish when we see sockeye jumpers entering the net. The company pays more money for sockeye and humpies are not really worth the effort."

I kept watching and tried to tell the difference but they were too far away for me to tell. Dad and Box both had no problem and I guessed that you just needed a lot of practice to be able to tell.

When we reached Telegraph Cove, Dad slowed the boat down and I was able to take a really good look around. This was another first for me and I wanted to remember everything so that I could tell Lavina about what I had seen.

The first thing I saw was a green building on pilings that looked similar to our cannery but much smaller. There were small cabins all along a wooden boardwalk. I saw a big building. As we came closer to the wharf , I was able to see and hear a huge saw buzzing. Dad said, "That is where the trees are made into lumber and where I will be working."

There were various types of boats in the water that I had never seen before. We reached a wharf where Dad and Box moored the *Kiona*. Dad said, "This will be our home for the next week."

I followed him down the ladder and went into the galley to see what Mom was doing. She had just finished putting our groceries away and asked me to get back on top of the boat again. I climbed back up as she handed me meat, vegetables and pop.

She said, "Ask your father where the cooler is and put all that stuff on ice." I turned to Dad and he pointed to a large white box that was leaning against a railing near the mast. I lifted up the lid and saw that it was half full of crushed ice. Dad told me not to eat the ice because it came from the fishing ice plant. This was something unusual and sort of innovative, I thought, as I put the supplies into the icebox / fridge.

While I was putting things away, my mind was running a mile a minute because I really wanted to ask Dad if I could go fishing with him the next time there was a salmon opening. I had seen so much in just this one day and wanted to learn more. I wanted to see how they made a set on sockeye and how it was different from beach seining at the river. I wanted to learn how to tell different salmon apart. There were just too many questions that I wanted answered.

It made me jealous when I thought of how Phillip boy had already been out gillnetting and already knew so much more then me.

I went back into the galley and was put on potato duty for supper. Mom was making hamburger patties while I peeled the spuds. After this was done, I went to explore the rest of the boat.

I went to the wheelhouse and saw that there were two beds that looked like bunk beds and two round windows that Dad said were called portholes. Walking out the wheelhouse door and along the side of the boat, I noticed a door and saw a tiny washroom, which smelled awful. Mom said that we used a bucket that was thrown overboard with a rope attached to get water. She said, "You pour the salt water in to make the toilet flush. The reason it smells bad is because the room is so small."

I ended up on the back deck and looked into the hatch and saw that it was empty. I knew that was where the fish were thrown when caught because I had rowed out to watch the boats delivering fish to the packers in the Bay.

Now that the engine was off, I had the courage to go down the ladder to the engine room. It had been way too scary and noisy for me to try when we were underway.

When I reached the bottom, I immediately felt claus-
trophobic. The engine seemed huge to me and only allowed a little room to walk by it. I inched my way past
and through another door.

I had reached the pointy end of the boat and saw
four more beds with mattresses buried a couple of inches down. Once again I had to run back to Dad and ask
a question. He said, "The mattresses are so low because
when it is rough, you will not fall out of bed as the boat
rocks back and forth. Box will be sleeping down there
this week"

This made me have second thoughts about asking
to go fishing for a couple of days on the family boat. I
then thought Box was brave to sleep down below all by
himself.

It was time to sit down and eat. I felt like Alice in
Wonderland. Everything was so close that you didn't have
to get up to get anything. Cups were hanging on hooks
above the table and plates were in slots so they wouldn't
fall over in rough weather. Just eating a meal was an adventure for me as I looked around the galley.

Mom asked me to do the dishes, when we were done
and I looked around for the faucets. She looked at me
funny trying not to laugh and then showed me how to use
the hand pump to get cold water. Mom asked me to pass
the kettle from the stove and she heated up the sink with
the hot water. I couldn't believe everything that I was
seeing and didn't mind doing the dishes for a change. It

only took me five minutes to wash, wipe and put everything back into its proper place because the galley was so small.

Dad and Box pulled out the crib board. The three of them started to play a game of three-handed cribbage. Mom said, "It's time to teach Honey how to count properly so she can make a fourth the next time that we are short a player." I felt really grown up then and closely watched them as they counted out fifteen two's and thirty-one's so that I could master this game of crib. It seemed like everyone in my family loved the game and there was no way that I was going to lose to my Dad. He was bigger than me and could push me around in soccer but I knew that in a game of cards that I could take him on and win. It would be time to turn the tables on him.

Little did I know that Dad was a demon at crib. He used that same jeering laugh in this and any game for that matter. He kept saying, "Are you sure you want to play that card?" to his opponents in an attempt to make them second-guess themselves.

Dad, Box and Mom played at least twenty hands of crib when I started to feel myself get tired. Mom looked over and noticed so she told me to get ready for bed. After washing up and brushing my teeth, she took me outside to the washroom (that Box called the can). It was fairly dark out and I looked up at the sky.

There were so many stars to see and I asked her why. Mom replied, " There are no house lights and streetlights over here like there is in the Bay. It makes them show up a lot brighter over here."

I quickly used the washroom and Mom already had the bucket full for me to use to flush the toilet. After going inside, Mom let me sleep on the top bunk. After struggling to get onto the bunk, I covered myself in the sleeping bag and looked out the small porthole at the stars.

I was totally amazed that they were so bright here in the Cove and we were only a mile or so away from the lights of the Bay. I could hear boats in the distance and felt the boat moving up and down with the tidal action inside the Cove.

It was nice and warm in the stateroom because the stove was just on the other side of the wall. I fell asleep looking at the stars and hearing light laughter and crib numbers being called out from the galley.

I woke up on the stateroom floor on a foam mattress and realized why I was allowed on the top bunk. It was easier for Dad to move me when they came to bed. There was no way that the two of them would have fit on one bunk bed.

I smelled coffee and bacon cooking. I ran around, if one can call it that trying to find clothes in the small-enclosed room. Dad and Box were already in their work clothes and had finished eating. It was still dark out but I could hear noise all around the boat. People were walking on the boardwalk and it was echoing throughout the small cove. Funny looking boats were moving around and the lights were already on in the sawmill.

Mom put a plate of bacon and eggs in front of me with hot chocolate on the side. Dad said, "I'll see you guys at lunch time."

I watched them jump off the boat from the galley porthole and wished that I could go and watch them work but Mom said that kids were not allowed in the workplace. After doing the dishes, I went to lie down for a while. I woke up to the hazy morning light.

I put a jacket on and asked if I could go on the top of the boat. Mom said, "Just be careful, I don't want to jump in the water for you." After promising to be very careful, I climbed the ladder. I sat on the chair by the wheel up top and watched the sun rise up over the tree line. There were so many different colors of blues and greens for me to see as the sun slowly brightened up the cove.

Even though the sun was up, there was condensation coming from my mouth and nose. The cold air didn't dampen my enthusiasm to see everything.

I was able to see many people walking around the sawmill, on logs in the water or in on boats doing their jobs. The *Kiona* was gently bobbing from the wave actions of other crafts in the water, which were those funny looking boats called dozers that pushed large logs around closer to the sawmill. Other men ran around with cork boots on those same logs and were tying them together. It was thrilling to watch how agile those loggers were on the logs and I kept expecting to see one of them fall in. I never did see anyone fall overboard.

I looked around the cove and saw some houses on rocky embankments and wondered how they were able to make a level home on those rocks. There was a large building in one corner and I figured that must be where the crew went to eat because I didn't see many boats around like the *Kiona*.

I watched as some men used a large forklift to maneuver a stack of lumber close to a boat tied up to the wharf. Other men tied ropes around it and hoisted it with a boom onto the boat. They gently swung it up and over the wharf then down onto the boat. Men quickly released the lines and the boom went back towards the wharf. This process was repeated until the boat deck was filled.

Men untied the boat's lines and the ship slowly passed by us. The skipper waved at me and I waved back. I watched until it passed the point and turned towards Port McNeill and Alert Bay.

I sat up top all day long, only leaving to go and get something to eat or to use the washroom. Everything was so new and exciting for me. Mom took me for a walk on the boardwalk. She introduced me to some kids who said they lived here with their parents in the houses on the hillside. Mom later told me that their parents owned the sawmill and I wondered where they went to school.

I ended up playing with these kids the whole time that we were there, while Mom visited their mothers. But, I was always happy to get back onto the *Kiona* so that I could watch the loggers at work.

Dad and Box took me out in the skiff after they finished work in the evenings and taught me how to properly row. I could barely move the oar but I enjoyed talking with them as they pointed out various things to me. Dad kept teasing me, saying, "Slow down, do you want to capsize us?" I knew that we were hardly moving but I got the hang of the proper rowing motion fairly fast.

The week came to an end much too quickly for me but I could hardly wait to get home to tell Lavina and Phil all about my adventure. I even learned not to gag every time that I had to use the can. As we pulled away from the wharf, my new friends waved good-bye to me and Dad tooted the horn at them.

After we were far enough away from the wharf, Dad opened up the engine and we chugged for home. I could see the Bay in the distance and was excited to be underway once again. I sat up top all the way home because I didn't know if I would be allowed to come over the next time Dad had to work.

It felt good to be heading home and as the sun dropped in the west, lights came on all over the Bay. I was excited to see some car headlights moving on the roads.

We hit the breakwater and Box leaped off the boat and tied both ends up securely. Dad cut the engine and I helped Mom pack up our clothes and sleeping bags. After struggling up the ramp with my hands full, I opened the car door and jumped in.

I begged to go and tell my cousins about everything I had seen but was told that it could keep until tomorrow. I went to bed hoping to fall asleep right away so that I wouldn't forget everything that I wanted to tell Lavina and Phil.

Chapter 28 - Fishing Days

Phillip boy and I were allowed to go food fishing with the family on the *Kiona*. It was a first for me because Phil had already gone and I was looking forward to the trip. We headed down the straits past Telegraph Cove. Once again, we were very close to the shore and we passed small houses in the middle of nowhere and I marveled that a family would want to stay somewhere so isolated.

I sat on top so I wouldn't miss anything. Uncle Ass and Oogie jumped into the skiff with their green rubber gear and gumboots on. Uncle Phil was standing by the big drum with his hands on some type of gears.

Uncle Pip slowed the boat down and went so close to the beach that I thought we were going to hit bottom. The bow of the boat was pushing kelp aside, then the skipper, yelled, "Let her go!"

All of a sudden I saw the skiff drop off the stern and Oogie threw something over that Phillip boy said was called the sea anchor. Uncle Phil released some gears that let the net go. The *Kiona* slowly turned from the shore and went straight out to the middle of the straits. Uncle Clarence rowed the skiff towards a rocky bluff while Oogie stood at the front.

Oogie jumped out onto the rocks and started to run, pulling the running line behind him. He raced to a tree with rope tied around it. He made some kind of knot then went back to the skiff where Uncle Ass was sitting and smoking.

While all this was going on, the drum was rattling as the lead line on the net turned over and over as it was being played out into the ocean. Once the net was cast out, Dad put a hook onto a clasp that Phillip boy explained was the tow line. I was sure glad Phillip boy was there to tell me what was going on. I would've been too scared to ask anyone else because they all seemed to have a job to do.

The *Kiona* made a slight turn and I sat on top looking over at the skiff, which was only a dot in the distance. I asked Phillip boy what was going on and he said, "We sit here with the net open until we see fish heading into it. Uncle Ass is called the skiff man, Oogie is the tie-up man, my Dad is drum man and your dad is the deckhand."

He then said, "Once we see fish, the skipper will start to tow and wave at Oogie to let the beach line go. Uncle will then have to row out the sea anchor. They will then head towards our boat. Don't get scared when we are towing towards the beach. The boat is going to go way over to one side."

I hoped that I wouldn't look scared because Phillip

boy wouldn't have said we would tilt over for no reason. Everyone on the *Kiona* and on the beach were staring at the water in front of the cork line and off into the distance hoping to spot jumpers. Dad came up and talked to the skipper for a short while. Uncle Phil was on the hatch smoking a cigarette and looking at the water. Phillip boy kept explaining to me what to expect as I asked a thousand and one questions.

I jumped when someone on deck yelled, "Inside, Inside!" Our skipper, Uncle Pip sped the engines up a notch or two and we started to move forwards. The net started to look like a giant letter "C" as we inched ahead. He made a turn towards the beach and I became a little afraid as I remembered what Phillip boy had said about the boat leaning over.

He waved at the beach and yelled, "Let her go!" I saw Oogie let the beach line go. Oogie ran to the skiff while holding the beach line and jumped in. Uncle Ass rowed backwards then turned towards the net that was along the beach. When they reached the sea anchor, Oogie pulled it into the skiff and Uncle started to really push on the oars. It looked like hard work as he made his way back towards the *Kiona*.

Uncle Phil was drumming in the net. He moved the levers in a smooth, fluid motion that kept the net coming in nice and even onto the drum. The boat did lean way over and I made sure to stand on the far side until I was sure that it wasn't going any further. I ran from side to side so that I could watch everything that was going on by the skiff, on the deck and at the drum.

Dad was at the bow of the seiner waiting for Oogie to hand him the beach line so that he could winch the other end of the net towards the boat. Phillip boy said, "Both sides come in then the rings will come up. Once the rings are up, the fish cannot dive under the net and we will have them trapped."

More things happened that I didn't really understand and Phillip boy wasn't there to explain because he was plunging at the end of the boat. Uncle Pip said, "Highball and get those rings on the hairpin, Joe."

I thought that it was funny that the rings came up then they let it go again. Phillip boy was back on top and he said, "The net is so close to the boat and up so high that this is just how it is done." I didn't understand but I guess they knew what they were doing. Somebody yelled, "Inside, sockeye!"

I was close enough to see jumpers this time and saw that sockeye really did jump straight up. The crew was happy because they knew we had caught something. Uncle Phil saw bubbles and now I saw what my uncles looked like when they were really excited. Phillip boy yelled in my ear that it was going to be a good set because the fish were gilling up and causing the bubbles.

Uncle Phil started doing a little jig and singing one of his songs. Skipper Pip said, "Get the brailer ready boys." I thought it was funny to hear my dad called a boy then

I realized I was going to see the crew brail. Standing up top, I could clearly see fish swimming around in circles throughout the net.

I felt tingly all over, watching all the fisherman so keyed up and animated. Everyone was talking and moving about the boat with some urgency but everything was going like clockwork.

The hatch was opened up and the brailer net was lowered into the water. Two men dipped and then it was lifted up and pushed over the hatch. One of them tugged on a rope and fish poured into the hatch. I saw a huge fish and asked Dad what it was. He said, "That's a spring salmon." It was the first time I had ever even saw a spring salmon.

I lost count of how many times they brailed. Finally they stopped and carried the last few rings to the back of the boat. I couldn't see what was going on from up top, then I heard fish slapping and jumping on the boat. There were hundreds of them sliding under the drum and Phillip boy was picking them up. He threw them into the hatch using a fish pick.

While Phil was doing this, the crew was getting the net and skiff ready for another set. After the deck was clear of fish, everyone manned their posts for the next set and we were off again.

Dad was using a pail and rope to get water and he washed the deck off. Blood, jellyfish, and kelp were all washed overboard. This continued on for the rest of the day until Uncle Pip figured we had enough sockeye to distribute to the crew's families and anyone else in the Bay who needed some fish.

Phillip boy kept trying to show me how to tell the salmon apart but I could only tell the difference between sockeye and springs because of the obvious size difference. I asked Phillip if fishing was always like this and he said, "No way. They get upset sometimes when something goes wrong if they are fishing for money. I think everyone is more relaxed because we are only food fishing right now. It's kind of like an organized chaos on deck when they screw up."

We headed back to the Bay and someone called on the radio phone to ask how much fish Uncle Pip was bringing in. I was shocked when he replied that we had between six-to-seven thousand pieces. I imagined everyone at home getting the totes and trucks ready to meet us at the breakwater later that day. Dad said, "We've caught that many fish and even more in one set when the sockeye are really running through the Straits."

I wished that I would be lucky enough one day to be on the boat when a really big set was caught because I could barely comprehend a set that had over twenty thousand fish inside the net.

I went down from the top of the boat to get a cup of tea. Oogie and Uncle Phillip were playing crib. I guess sitting on top was old news to them and they were quite content sipping coffee and playing cards. I went back up top and listened to Dad and Uncle Pip talk but wasn't really paying attention because I was too busy looking at the beautiful scenery all around me. It was something that the men in the family were lucky enough to see every time they went out fishing or hunting and I wasn't about to miss one moment of it.

When we docked, my family used the boat to move the fish up onto the dock with the brailer. I stayed there while they unloaded the valuable fish to family and others. It seemed like the hatch would never be emptied out but I didn't get bored while watching all that fish going to homes in the Bay.

People were asking for twenty, thirty, forty and fifty pieces for their families and no one was turned aside once the crew's family had gotten their share of the sockeye. The humpies and coho were taken for smoking, the sockeye for canning and barbecuing and the big smileys (spring salmon) were even grabbed by different people that had a use for them.

I knew that we were going to be busy for the next two days doing fish behind the Big House once again but was very glad that I was able to see how seine fishing was done.

Chapter 29 - Phil Moves On

Uncle Charley-horse and Auntie Annie were building a new house to the right of the Big House and they were really excited. Phillip boy and I played around the house whenever the men were not working on the new home. It looked pretty tiny to us as the foundation was laid out but it seemed to expand as the walls went up. Toomuch was really looking forward to moving into the new house.

I was happy for my uncle and aunt because of the new house but at the same time I was unhappy. Phillip boy and his family would be moving out of the Big House and into the small apartment across the Council Hall once Uncle Charley-horse moved his family out of it and into their new house.

I could see that Granny Axu was having the same mixed emotions that I was having. She wanted her kids to do well and have a home but at the same time it hurt her when someone else moved out of the Big House.

They would only be a two or three-minute walk away but I was used to having Phillip boy around and he was like another brother to me. I wouldn't be able to just walk down the hall and talk with him if something was bothering me, if I was just lonely or just needed someone to talk to about practically anything that came up.

The day finally came when both families packed up and moved into the new dwellings. It felt like I was losing something and the Big House felt empty without that one family. I knew that things would change in my life and I didn't want that to happen but I had to accept them. It was a fact of life that I had to deal with but knowing it and having to accept it were two things that I was having a very hard time dealing with.

The end result was that Phillip boy and I took turns spending weekends with each other every chance we had. It may seem funny for a boy and a girl to be so close but that is just how it was. Phillip boy always got me to ask Auntie Eddie if he could stay with me because it was harder for her to say no to me then it was to him. We think she thought that my parents were getting tired of him staying over but the reality of it was that it kept me from bugging Mom and Dad to let me stay with him at the house on the beach.

I missed him being around so much that I would race down the stairs every time the phone rang just in case Phillip boy was calling me. I mastered getting down the seventeen stairs in three giant steps and spun around the corner then on down the hall in less then ten seconds. All my friends knew that if I was the only one home, they should let the phone ring at least seven times because that is about the time it took me to get to the phone from the upstairs apartment.

This must have contributed to our always being in some sort of shape year round no matter what the weather looked like outside.

The next ones to move out were Uncle Urban and Auntie Libby. They moved over to Port McNeill into one of the small homes that the logging companies supplied for the workers because it was more convenient for Uncle Urban than having to commute back and forth. This affected Granny A$\underline{x}$u deeply because Auntie "Bessie" was her baby daughter and her daughter Judy wasn't too far behind in her affections. This wasn't as hard on me because I didn't really play with Judy and she was a lot younger then me but I could see that Granny was hurting when they packed out their belongings. Joe and I were moved into Auntie Libby's room to share it while Cory stayed in the apartment with Mom and Dad.

The last family to move out was Uncle Dayu and Auntie Nora. They were building their own version of a Big House, where Uncle Dayu planned on moving his parents in with his immediate family. Their new house was also a few minutes away but the house seemed so empty every time part of the family moved out. Lavina had moved back home with her family behind the Council Hall. George came and went whenever he felt like living with us or with his parents. Each move caused some happiness, unhappiness and stress to everyone involved.

Joe ended up getting Eva's old room at the top of the stairs next door to me while Cory continued to stay with our parents still. Uncle Ass moved into Uncle Phillip's old bedroom and his three sons moved into Uncle Dayu's room. Granny Axu spent the majority of her time on the fold out couch in the living room more and more. Times were changing, we were still a tightly knit family but the old feeling of the Big House was forever changed in my mind.

Our berry picking days with Granny Axu became fewer and fewer because she wasn't as agile as she used to be. I'm not saying that she wasn't still very active for someone her age. She still walked up the stairs to call Joe or me to do something for her or to call us to the telephone if we hadn't heard the phone ring. She was full of life at the potlatches, her church meetings and her native crafts.

Granny Pearlie had moved to Vancouver to live and my Auntie Connie didn't like it down in the "Big City." She called and asked my Mom if she could come and live with us. Mom told her that it was no problem and I looked forward to her coming to stay with us. Auntie Connie was only two or three years older then me and I hoped that she could fill the void left by everyone who had left the Big House.

Connie called and said that she would be in on the *M. V. Island Princess* that evening and I was really excited. Dad drove me down to the government wharf in his new big yellow Chevrolet Impala to meet the ferry after dinner.

Connie was waving at me from the boat as it docked. It seemed to take forever for the crew to put the ramp down for Connie to get off of the *Island Princess*. She walked down the ramp and handed over a six pack of Crush Cream Soda to me because we couldn't buy it in the Bay and she knew that it was my favorite drink at the time.

Things were looking up already. We loaded her bags into the trunk of the car and went home. I helped her unpack her stuff into the room that we would be sharing. Connie dressed and acted like a young lady. I think that Mom hoped that she would rub off on me to end my wild days with Phillip boy and other male cousins.

Connie fit in with us in the Big House immediately and got along with my older cousins. And she did settle me down a bit.

Chapter 30 - School Daze

We had been working really hard on our carnival night at the high school. There was going to be a dunking pond, craft tables, baked goods, dart throws, and many other fun things happening at the school that night. It was a huge success with a lot of money raised by the school student council. We went back to school thrilled with ourselves because everyone had contributed to the event.

Imagine the surprise of the student council when they were told they would not have a say in how the money would be used, after all the work the students had put into the carnival. A future leader in my mind, named Renee, decided to stage a walkout in protest. Grades 8-10 left the school after lunch and never went back to make sure the point was made that the student council should have a say in regard to the dollars made.

Everyone of the students walked down the hill in one huge unified group and it was quite the sight to see. I kept expecting to see the Principal come and try to force us back to class but that never happened.

It just so happened to be my birthday that day and almost everyone near my age ended up at the Big House talking over the students' options. Mom set to work cooking up more spaghetti for my dinner because almost everyone stayed for my birthday supper.

I had no political aspirations but was enjoying everything that was being said by the student executive to the people at the house. Cousins were saying radical things. The reality was that they were happy not to be in school.

That was the last big family birthday dinner I would ever have in the Big House. The student council ended up negotiating the right to have a say in the use of the carnival money.

Chapter 31 - A Sister Arrives

One of our cousins moved into the Big House during the last few years of my life there at the end of one hot summer. She took over the spare room next to the bathroom on the main floor.

As I said earlier, Granny A<u>x</u>u was still agile enough to handle the stairs to our apartment. She came up the stairs and into our living room calling for my Mom with some excitement in her voice.

She said, "Come downstairs, Kunn. There is something thing wrong." Mom followed her down the stairs as Gran was speaking in kwaḵwala telling her what was happening. I didn't understand what was being said but could tell that there was something in the air because of the sense of urgency in the tone of their voices.

Mom came back upstairs and said that she had to take my cousin to the hospital. She was going to have a baby. I sat there in shock because I had no idea that she was even pregnant.

My mom wasn't gone that long before she came home

and said that my cousin had a baby girl. The baby had to be delivered with forceps then Mom proceeded to tell me what forceps were used for because I didn't have a clue what it meant. Mom said the baby girl was born with no hair and had a fair sized egg on her forehead from the forceps pulling her out of her mother's womb.

We all looked forward to the day that she would return to the Big House from the hospital. I had just started babysitting for small babies and enjoyed it. The day came and we all crowded around the baby who was named Laureen. She looked so tiny but cute. The bump slowly went down on her forehead that we barely even noticed it. All we saw were her smiles and baby giggles that made everyone in the house want to pick her up and carry her.

Our cousin was going to Victoria to take a course and asked my parents if they would be willing to take care of Laureen for six weeks. Mom said yes right away and I don't even know if she consulted Dad.

Our apartment was in an upheaval as Mom prepared an area for the baby. She went on a shopping spree to get clothes. It made her really happy to have another baby since the three of us were well on our way to some sort of an immature independence.

Dad tried not to become too attached because he knew that he would miss Laureen when we had to give her back to her real mother in six weeks. The baby had too much going for her though because day by day, I saw Dad weakening and falling for her.

Instead of just rushing up the stairs for Hockey Night in Canada, Dad now sprinted home to come and play with the baby. Dad loved kids so much and knew that Mom had no intention of having another baby any time soon. Laureen was quickly given a nickname like almost everyone else in the family.

Her new name became Gin-Gin and became shortened to Gin. The baby softened Joe and I up in many ways because our fights became fewer and far between. It may be that we were finally growing up and were learning to get along with each other. We even quit teasing Cory and didn't call her Charming girl as much.

The six weeks were nearly over and I saw both my parents walking around with worried looks on their faces. We had formed a very tight emotional bond with Gin.

Our cousin called and asked if we could keep Gin a bit longer because she had to do something else in Victoria. The answer in my mind was automatic but I didn't know what was going through Mom and Dad's minds.

They talked it over and both decided that even though it would hurt when Gin would have to go back, they decided more time with her was better then no time at all. I broke into a huge grin when they told us their decision.

Besides getting Gin for a few more weeks, our family was given a chance to get a home from the band. Mom was looking forward to it but I knew that Dad was worried about how Granny Aҳu would feel when she heard how soon we might be moving out of the Big House.

Our family was given the option of picking homes that were already built or waiting to design a style of our own. Mom chose the second option, which made Dad happy. It meant that we would have to wait for a lot to be cleared and a cement foundation to be poured.

All I remember thinking is that we were getting a home with four bedrooms and a washroom for our family and ours alone. There would always be enough hot water and I wouldn't have to run as far to answer the phone. I wouldn't have to refill the oil canister and I would be living fifty yards away from the soccer field. Phillip boy's second new house would be on the same block, which was another added bonus.

I was going to be sixteen within the next year or so and it just seemed right that we were getting a new house.

Dad was still thinking about how our moving out would affect Granny Axu and he wasn't looking forward to the moving day. I don't think that any of us kids realized how much our moving into a new home might disturb Granny Axu.

When the house was almost finished, Dad and Uncle Ass went to install the kitchen cupboards by themselves. The rest of us were painting the trim for the living room while Gin lay in her car seat in the new kitchen watching the two adults putting up the cupboards.

They argued for over an hour about which end to start from. I don't know who won the argument but the last cupboard didn't fit. The two of them blamed each other much like Joe and I did whenever we disagreed, then the two of them started to remove all the cupboards.

Another humourous argument started as they tried to figure out a way to get all the cupboards to fit. Dad said, "I told you we should've gone right to left."

Uncle Ass replied, "No, No, you didn't! I was the one that said we should've went right to left but no, no, you never listen to the smarter one."

This started the two of them for another half an hour or so about how to do it properly. Gin just lay there and stared at the two of them joining in the laughing because she thought it was meant for her. Joe, Cory and I just rolled our eyes because now we knew where our stubborn behavior came from along with our very strong opinions about always being right in any arguments.

Dad and Uncle Ass finally were able to put the cupboards up before midnight but the argument never ceased throughout the drilling and nailing. We all went home and had a good laugh at the two carpenters in the family.

The deadline for our cousin to come and pick up Gin was rolling around once again. Tension gripped the whole family. Mom talked with Dad and they decided to ask our cousin if they could adopt Gin. Mom called her in Victoria and asked her if adoption was a possibility. She said that she would think about it and get back to them.

It seemed like forever before she called back. I know that she was doing a lot of soul searching because she knew how much we had all fallen in love with Gin. It was not a decision she could make without someone being hurt whatever the decision. I know that she also cared deeply for Gin.

She called back and was almost crying but said that she realized that Gin would probably be better off with us and said yes. Mom told Dad and it looked like he wanted to cry but I don't think anyone of us could have punched that huge grin off his face. Our parents were now going to have four children, which was a perfect number in Kwagu'ł culture.

The day came when the house was almost ready and we slowly started to move some personal belongings from the Big House into the new building.

I finally noticed that Dad didn't have that normal bounce in his walk and that is when it hit me that he was concerned for Granny A<u>x</u>u. The move was hurting him because he knew that Granny didn't really want us to move out because that only left Uncle Ass, his boys and some distant relatives living with her. It seemed like every time something good happened to anyone in our family, something else would counterbalance the joy with the sorrow.

The Big House was no longer going to be my home anymore and I realized that I had been so lucky to grow up in what was very similar to one of the last Kwagu'ł Big Houses for the most formative years of my life.

I came to understand that the days in the Big House had made each and everyone of us care about our extended family, and that caring would last for the rest of my life. I may not have understood what Granny A<u>x</u>u was saying to me half the time but she had been a major force in my life and would continue to be.

My mind, raced when I pondered what we would be losing and gaining and this allowed me to see why Dad was so upset. I thought back on all my memories; not all of them were happy but they were what made me the person that I am.

As I went to sleep in my new home that night, I am not ashamed to say that I shed a few tears of sadness because I knew I would not be able to give my own future children the same kind of upbringing that we had all received from the experience of living in the Big House.

Conclusion

Granny A<u>x</u>u's son Clarence's (Uncle Ass) family eventually married and moved out of the Big House. Granny's youngest daughter Libby Wattinger moved home when Granny was unable to look after herself any longer.

The 'Na<u>m</u>gis First Nation built Granny A<u>x</u>u a one-level home in 1986 that was equipped to handle her special needs. Some family members used the Big House for a few years after she moved out but it was much too large and expensive to maintain. It was abandoned and sat empty for many years.

It caught fire late one night and vandalism was thought to be the cause. All that is left to remind the family of the Big House is a big empty lot with a white rose bush beside the road that blooms every May.

Cousin Harold Alfred has the right to build on the empty lot when he decides to move back home.

Granny A<u>x</u>u became a long term patient at St. Georges Hospital after Auntie Libby could no longer give the necessary care. Granny passed away at the age of 103 on December 11, 1992.

Her last words to family at St Georges Hospital were:
"Love one another and help one another."

Granny A̱xu

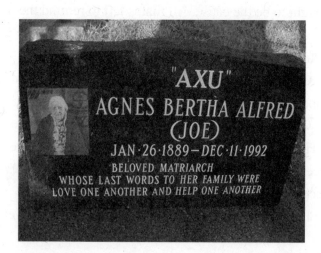

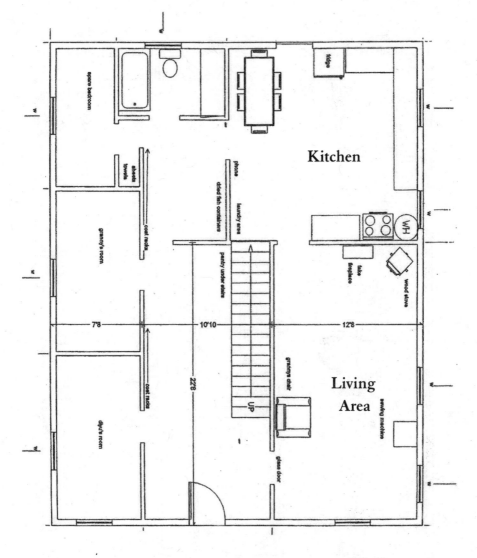

Big House Main Floor

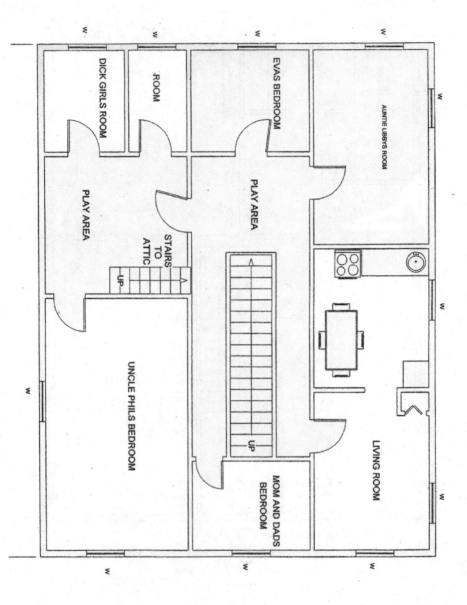

Big House Third Floor

Dorothy, George, Eva

Back row, left to right: Pip, Alvin, Flora, Nora, Lena, Phillip, Jimmy.

Front row, left to right: Allan, Granny, Libby, Clarence

Our Malibu Wave

Joe with his pooltable

Granny and Grampa

Grampa Moses, Clarence, Granny, Allan, Libby

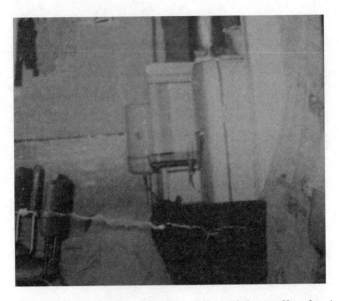

Our apartment and the dreaded five gallon oil drum off to the right

Joe on his tractor behind the Big House. Clothes can be seen on the back porch

Newly Built Traditional Big House after the original Traditional Big House burnt down

Traditional Big House

Some of the Olympic participants. Joe, Oogie, Harold, Honey,
Bruce, Charlene, Derek.

Some of the Dick family: back row, Nora, Dayu;
front, Tina Tidi, Art

Gramps, Granny and Joe after he was baptized

Joe, Cory and Honey

Dad playing with Frank Cook before Longo showed up

One of the many games played by family members.
Left to right; Honey, Dad, Libby, Eva

Left to right: Honey, Deane Wadhams, Wendy Peterson

Lavina, Honey, Joe, and Harry

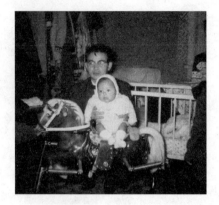

When the Lead horse was still brand new; Dad and Joe

Mom and Dad on his Archie Bunker chair

Honey with one of her many trophies

Cory packing Laureen "Gin-Gin"

Our Big House empty and before the fire

Printed in Canada